LIFE IN SCOTLAND
since 1603

NORMAN NICHOL

Adam & Charles Black · London

Drumlanrig Castle, a seventeenth-century country house, was built for William Douglas, 1st Duke of Queensberry. (He occupied it for only one day, horrified at the enormous cost.)

LIFE IN SCOTLAND since 1603

First published 1975 by A. & C. Black Ltd.
4, 5 & 6 Soho Square, London W1V 6AD

© 1975 A. & C. Black Ltd.

ISBN 0 7136 1455 2

Companion volume :
LIFE IN SCOTLAND until 1603
ISBN 0 7136 1454 4

*COVER ILLUSTRATIONS : colour prints
of starting a stage coach and of washerwomen ;
'Pitlessie Fair' by David Wilkie ; a colliery
notice ; an advertisement for an early washing
machine ; an oil rig in the North Sea.*

Filmset and printed in Great Britain
by BAS Printers Limited, Wallop,
Hampshire

Contents

Macmillan's Bicycle 1839 – the first to look at all like the modern version.

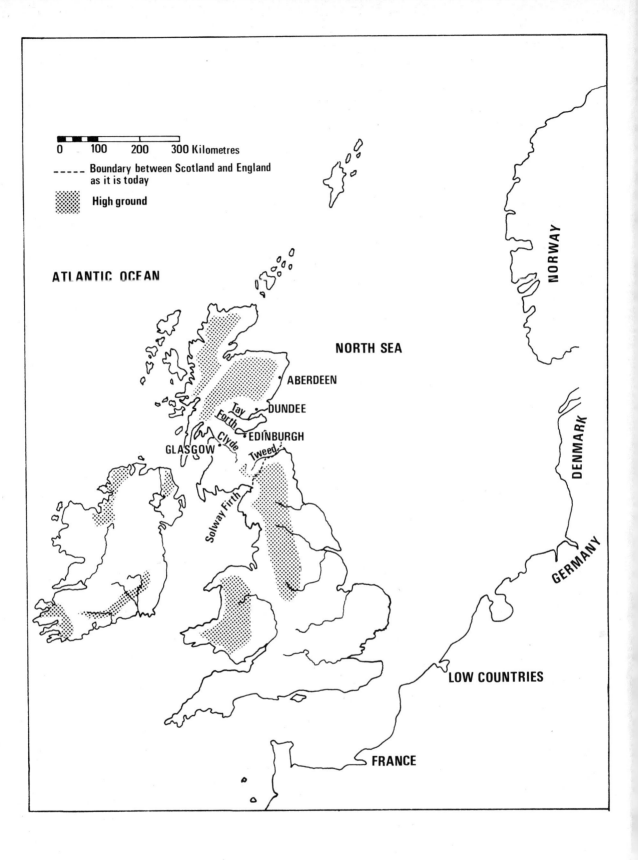

0   100   200   300 Kilometres

----- Boundary between Scotland and England
as it is today

High ground

ATLANTIC OCEAN

NORTH SEA

ABERDEEN

Tay
Forth   DUNDEE

Clyde   EDINBURGH

GLASGOW

Tweed

Solway Firth

NORWAY

DENMARK

GERMANY

LOW COUNTRIES

FRANCE

17 SEVENTEENTH CENTURY

A courtier, Robert Carey, rode north from London in 1603 to tell James VI of Queen Elizabeth's death. People marvelled at the speed of his journey, because he covered the 640 kilometres in only sixty hours.

Nowadays the journey by air from London to Edinburgh takes sixty minutes. Living, working and travelling in seventeenth-century Scotland was still very different from what it is today.

The sketches made by John Slezer in 1693 show the differences very clearly. They picture a land of naked hills and rough moorland, with tiny burghs clustered round old churches and castles. The roads that link the burghs are only rough tracks.

Scotland was still a land of country folk. Ninety per cent of the population were peasant farmers, living in one-roomed hovels built with their own hands, wearing clothes of homespun wool and linen.

The central lowlands were the richest area, with wheat, oats and barley grown in the Lothians and Clydesdale, dairy farming in Ayrshire and fruit-growing in the sheltered Clyde valley. Edinburgh and Glasgow, market towns as well as centres for spinning and weaving, were the two largest burghs.

John Slezer was a Dutchman serving in Scotland as a captain in the army. His book of sketches 'Theatrum Scotiae' was published in 1693.

Slezer's view of Dumbarton Rock. Sportsmen are fowling and fishing by the Clyde. The only buildings in sight are the ancient castle on the Rock and a couple of farm cottages.

Slezer shows a peaceful farming scene at Brechin, countryfolk leading a laden horse. The field is ridged with wide plough furrows beginning to be overgrown by weeds and scrub.

Women washing clothes at Dundee, a sight to be seen in any part of Scotland. Two are stamping out the dirt with their bare feet – which, in winter, would be blue with cold.

Bride and bridegroom lead the dancing in De Wit's painting of a Lowland Wedding (1684). The men wear flat bonnets, long coats and breeches while the women have plaids over their heads and shoulders. The man in the right foreground sports a large basket-hilted sword.

On both the east and west coasts there were herring ports, Greenock on the west and Anstruther, Crail and Dunbar on the east. Musselburgh and Leith were famous for shell-fish and oysters.

Coal was mined along the Forth, round Glasgow and at Irvine, and was used for the salt pans at Saltcoats and Preston-pans, as well as for glass making, soap boiling and other small industries in the burghs.

The Border lands were less populated, for the great sheep farms needed fewer workers, and in Galloway much land was given over to horse and cattle breeding. Dumfries, Wigtown, Peebles and the old Border towns of Jedburgh, Kelso and Melrose were the chief centres, while Portpatrick linked the south-west area with Ireland.

Some of Slezer's drawings show low-landers at their daily work, farmers in their fields, herdsmen with cattle and sheep, women at their wash tubs, fisher-men netting salmon and packmen leading laden horses. Others show comfortable-

Three men hunting duck at Culross. One shoots, one collects the fallen birds and a third sits comfortably smoking a churchwarden pipe, with a boathook for birds that fall in the water.

Nobles hunting deer in the Duke of Hamilton's Low Park. A full century was to pass before coal mines and ironworks made Lanarkshire an industrial area.

looking burgesses enjoying an afternoon at fishing and fowling.

Another drawing shows high life in the Duke of Hamilton's parks. For most people shooting had taken the place of deer hunting but the greatest aristocrats still had their deer parks. Wearing plumed hats, flowing coats and long riding boots, they ride at a stag chased up by hounds and beater.

Yet another drawing shows an assembly of nobility at a great country mansion. The gentlemen wear wigs and low-crowned hats, long many-buttoned coats, kneebreeches and ribboned shoes. They carry swords as a sign of their rank. The ladies wear long dresses with panniers and elbow-length sleeves, long curls and little caps.

The courtyard is full of private coaches. Wealthy people liked having a private coach to show off their wealth though they could only use it when the roads were dry, in the summer.

Working people dressed more plainly, even on festive occasions, in clothes made from homespun linen and wool.

An aristocratic gathering at Thirlestane Castle outside Lauder, Berwick. The garden is formal in the French style and the costume is that of the nobility and the wealthy.

Private carriages at Falkland, Fife. Slezer makes the big coaches look attractive but they had no springs and the almost impassable roads soon shattered wheels and axles.

De Wit's Highland Wedding shows the guests dressed much the same as in the Lowland Wedding, except that the men are wearing tartan trews.

Three methods of transporting goods : packhorse, back-pack and bundle. All three travellers are carrying stout walking sticks. In the background of Slezer's picture is Culross Abbey.

Slezer's pictures do not include the highlands. Beyond the highland line there were no roads and no towns. The highlanders lived a separate way of life in their bleak and mountainous country: hunting, fishing, grazing sheep and cattle, and tilling their small stony fields. The Gaelic-speaking clansmen travelled long distances to markets at Inverness, Perth, Dunkeld and Crieff.

South-east of the highland line life was more varied. The flat lands round Inverness, the Black Isle, and the plains of Moray and Aberdeen provided good farming land, such as the lands about the Tay. Here harvests ripened quickly and farmers grew enough to sell their grain to other parts of Scotland as well as to the

Continent. Aberdeen and Dundee had grown into big ports of over 10 000 people. Aberdeen had a prosperous woollen industry and Dundee, like Perth and Montrose, was a centre for the linen trade. Both the Don and the Tay were salmon-fishing rivers.

One of Slezer's most interesting views is a sketch of Scotland's biggest seventeenth-century city, Edinburgh. It shows how the farm rigs go right up to the waters of the North Loch, where Edinburgh's Princes Street and Gardens lie today.

The sketch was made from the village of Dean, now swallowed up in central Edinburgh and overlaid with houses. Slezer saw it as a hamlet on the Water of Leith, a jumble of stone houses and cottages set among gardens and haystacks. Down at the water's edge a double water wheel worked a waulk mill, where cloth was finished off and felted.

Edinburgh was already facing a problem of overcrowding. The burgh now filled the long rocky ridge stretching from the Castle to the Netherbow Port and the population was packed into steep wynds branching like herring bones from the High Street, as can be seen in an old map of 1647.

To house more people builders raised tenements up to eleven storeys high but usually of six or seven storeys. Rich and poor lived in the same block.

The best houses were two or three storeys up, well away from the noise and dirt of the streets but not too far to climb. Rich lawyers or nobles lived in these. Shopkeepers and craftsmen lived above, and poor people on the ground level or in the cellars.

Slezer's view of Edinburgh and the village of Dean on the Water of Leith. A watermill was built nearby in the time of David I and successive mills stood on the spot till recently.

John Slezer's job was to inspect armouries and powder magazines. His sketch of Edinburgh Castle shows a soldier's grasp of the fortifications of the castle.

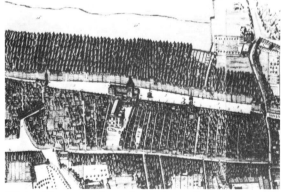

This old map, 1647, shows how the seventeenth-century burgh of Edinburgh now consisted of a solid mass of housing on each side of the High Street.

The painting by Roderick Chambers of the Craftsmen of Holyroodhouse Palace, 1721, shows each carrying out his special task. Reading from left to right: sievewright, slater, glazier, cooper, mason, wright, bowmaker, painter, plumber and upholsterer.

Some lawyers and burgesses lived in the Cowgate or Westerbow areas, which they could reach by horse and carriage. Even there they were content with a house of three rooms and a kitchen. Lord Kennet was a famous lawyer but at night his children and their nurse slept in his study, and the maidservant slept under a cupboard in the kitchen. The other two rooms were the lawyer's bedroom and the drawing room.

By 1690 the Burgh Council bought up other lands to build on. These included the neighbouring burgh of Canongate and also High Riggs, the Pleasance, North Leith and Portsburgh.

Seventeenth-century builders had no idea of sanitation and visitors to Edinburgh learned to dread the sound of the Town drum at ten o'clock. This was the signal for women to tip sewage and slops out of the upstairs windows, with a warning shout of 'Gardyloo'.

Pedestrians shouted: 'Haud your haund!' or dived for shelter, but nothing could stop the terrible and deadly stench known as 'the flowers of Edinburgh'.

In 1687 the Council hired twenty two-horse carts to take away refuse every night except Sunday. The filth often contaminated the water supply and water from the wells contained a murderous collection of germs.

Few of Edinburgh's 30 000 residents were burgesses. Many people worked as porters, water carriers, milk vendors,

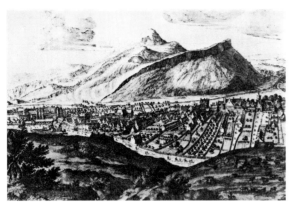

Canongate burgh immediately below Edinburgh (see the map on page 85) was much less crowded. Many houses still had large gardens.

Wealthy merchants such as Heriot and the Hutchesons left money to help orphans of members of the Guild. Above: Heriot's School today.

A street view of Paul's Work which was a large building enclosing an inner courtyard. The Town Council and private individuals supported it with their money – for a while.

Napier's Bones: the first calculating machine, invented by John Napier (1550–1617) who also invented logarithms. The two inventions led eventually to the modern slide rule.

hawkers, drovers, carters, servants, sedan chairmen, labourers or link-boys – who carried torches and guided people through the dark streets.

An early eighteenth-century visitor, Captain Burt, described the Edinburgh caddies (porters and guides) as 'wretches that lie in rags upon the streets'.

When they could get no work the poor lived on charity. The Town Council gave licences allowing people to beg and opened a Poor House, Paul's Work, in 1633. Kirk Sessions also collected alms and doled them out to the poor.

Members of the Guilds looked after their own poor, for every member paid a contribution to Guild Funds. Rich merchants such as George Heriot left money to found hospitals (orphanages) for the orphan children of burgesses.

When Daniel Defoe (journalist and author of *Robinson Crusoe*) visited Edinburgh in 1707 he reported it was as bad as London for shoplifters, house-robbers and pickpockets, even though it had a Town Guard of two companies of armed and uniformed watchmen.

Seventeenth-century painting of Lady Mary Erskine by George Jamesone (born in Aberdeen 1587). She wears a lace collar, starched ruff and dress with elaborate sleeves.

Self portrait by seventeenth-century painter Scougal shows the fashion of the day : carefully trimmed moustache, clipped beard and dark clothing with white collar and cuffs.

Daniel Defoe thought Edinburgh a fine city, in spite of its dirt and smell. He compared its beautiful stone buildings with the 'paper-built' cities of England and especially admired its High Street, 'the longest and best-built' in Europe.

The centre of city life was the Market Cross, where the trumpeter regularly blew for silence and the herald read out public announcements. The Cross was busiest between eleven and one o'clock, for merchants, lawyers and other gentlemen gathered in the open to discuss business and politics and the news of the day.

Women shopped for herbs, fruit and vegetables in the open market held every morning in the High Street. For other goods they went to the special walled markets, the Meal Market, Flesh Market, Poultry Market or Butter Market. Once a week they could buy drapery, woollens and linen cloth in the Landmarket. Rich people who wanted luxury goods ordered them from the merchants who had warehouses full of goods in the West Bow, and who supplied all the tradesmen's needs in the way of timber, iron goods, paint, oil, dyes, drugs and so on.

When he visited Glasgow in the same year, Defoe found it 'one of the cleanliest, most beautiful' and best built cities in Great Britain'. It had been rebuilt after a fire in 1677 with wide streets and stone houses all planned the same size. The lower storeys rested on arched columns,

Another view of the Old Bridge, Glasgow – it can be compared with the picture on page 61. This was the only bridge until the Broomielaw was built late in the eighteenth century.

A seventeenth-century lowland woman, with long skirt, linen apron, short cloak and starched collar. The sober costume almost certainly reflects the influence of the Kirk.

Solid seventeenth-century houses with outside forestairs line Castle Street, Glasgow. Beyond rises the Cathedral tower. The costume of the woman at the market stall and of the pedestrians shows that the picture was not made until the early nineteenth century.

providing space for booths and market stalls.

Glasgow had the reputation of being the godliest city in Scotland. Its Church organisation gives us a good idea of how the Kirk ruled people's lives in other burghs also.

The Reformed Church was modelled on John Calvin's Church in Geneva. Ministers in Glasgow wanted to build up a god-fearing community and worked hand in glove with the magistrates to make sure that citizens lived sober and upright lives.

The cathedral was taken over to house Presbyterian congregations. The choir became the Inner High Kirk, the nave the Outer High Kirk and the crypt the Laigh or Barony Kirk. Rows of stones served as seats in the great cavernous building, until wooden forms were provided for the men. Women were expected to bring their own folding stools.

When Charles I, and later Charles II, tried to model the Scottish Kirk on the Church of England, people were very angry. This drawing shows the 'Arch Prelate' of St. Andrews being attacked while in the pulpit. Many noblemen and their followers signed the National Covenant in 1638, declaring their support for the Scottish Kirk.

RANGE OF HOUSES IN CASTLE STREET, OPPOSITE THE BARONY CHURCH, PARTLY TAKEN DOWN IN 1844.

The Low Corner House was the Hangman's Abode.   Prebendal Manse of the Lord of Provan.

Rotten Row, Glasgow. A prebendal manse was a house owned by a large city church and occupied by one of its ministers. Wealthy men sometimes gave a house to the Kirk.

The ministers preached long sermons, often terrifying the congregation by describing how God would punish the wicked. Sometimes they were not so fiery and people dozed off. Beadles had orders to use their long sticks to lift women's headshawls to make sure that they stayed awake.

In the reign of Charles I the whole country rose in rebellion when the king tried to change the Scottish Kirk to match the Church of England.

After the Civil War the ministers and magistrates punished Sabbath-breaking very severely. Women must not gossip or draw water from the well in service time. No buying or selling was allowed. Ministers and elders scolded those lingering after the service to gossip by the bridge and Seizers arrested idle strollers. The schoolmaster had orders to punish boys found playing outdoors.

Respectable families attended kirk twice a day, ate a cold dinner in silence and then sat in a darkened room. Shutters were opened to give just enough light for reading the Scriptures.

Absentees from church had to pay fines or stand dressed only in a sackcloth robe at the pillar of repentance.

The Kirk disapproved of Christmas festivities and Glasgow Kirk Session speedily banned the custom of pipers touring the streets on St. Thomas's Eve (22 December). They also forbade all Christmas plays, guisings, pipings, drink and other 'superstitious exercises'.

They also kept a severe eye on people's private behaviour. They scolded husbands and wives who quarrelled, frowned on dancing, piping and drumming at weddings and christenings, and they appointed 'Noters' who reported those who swore or blasphemed. The fine was twelve pence.

Kirk Sessions had the right to punish misbehaviour in all sorts of ways. There were penances, when the offender stood at the Church door or by a pillar, barefooted, often wearing a white sheet with a paper fastened on their brows to show what they were guilty of. Kirk Sessions sometimes fined culprits or ordered them to be put in the jougs or branks, or sent them to the Correction House in Rotten Row, to be fed on bread and water and whipped daily.

Slezer's view of Haddington shows the rough track which was the main road through to Edinburgh, the unfenced rigs and the huge church, the 'Lamp of Lothian'.

Presbyterian reformers and their congregations disapproved of the decorated churches of the Middle Ages. Lyne Church, near Peebles, is built in the plain post-Reformation style.

Two forms of punishment. Left : jougs – an iron neck ring attached to a pillar. Right : branks – an iron cage which could be fitted round the head and over the tongue.

A banner carried by Covenanters in 1679: they had made a 'covenant' (promise) to God, to uphold what they believed to be the true faith.

The Kirk kept up this kind of control over people's lives right into the eighteenth century, particularly in the southwest. Charles II (1660–85) appointed bishops and took away the right of congregations to elect their own ministers. Three hundred ministers gave up their kirks and held open-air services, coventicles, rather than obey. They risked torture and death and so did the congregations who supported them. Sentries were posted to give warning of the approach of the king's troops.

The Covenanters, as the rebels were called, were ready to fight if necessary. In June 1679 a group of armed Lanarkshire farmers defeated a troop of professional

In 1679 a group of Lanarkshire and Ayrshire farmers (40 mounted and 200 on foot) defeated a larger force of dragoons at Drumclog, near Strathaven, Lanark. (This success encouraged Covenanters to resist a royal army at Bothwell Brig. But there they ran out of ammunition and were defeated.)

soldiers led by Graham of Claverhouse at Drumclog.

The persecution of Covenanters ended when William and Mary became rulers in 1690 and the Presbyterian Church set up again under the rule of its General Assembly.

At times the strong religious feeling of the seventeenth century led to hideous crimes. The Scots were the worst persecutors of supposed witches in the whole of Europe – over 4000 died in witch-hunts in the seventeenth and early eighteenth centuries.

Persecution went on until 1728, when the last execution of a 'witch' took place at Dornoch and an old woman was strangled on a charge of having turned her daughter into a pony. By that time educated people had lost their fear of witchcraft and as more people learned to read their belief in spells and magic died away.

The spread of education was due to the Kirk, which set great store on every person being able to read the word of God set down in the Bible. As early as 1560 the Scots reformers had published a plan for a network of schools and colleges in 'The Book of Discipline' which said that there should be a school in every parish.

In 1696 the Scottish parliament passed an Act which said landowners and tenants had to pay a stent and provide a school in each parish. They also had to appoint a schoolmaster and pay him a salary of 100 marks (£5.11s) a year.

This was a very low salary, even though the children also paid a small fee every quarter. Schoolmasters had to do other work to eke out their incomes. They acted as parish clerks, precentors and sometimes even as gravediggers.

People accused of witchcraft had little chance of escape. Many were tortured till they confessed.

Swimming a witch: anyone guilty would float.

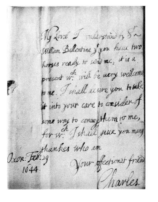

An example of the handwriting of the time. A letter written by Charles II, as 14 year old Prince of Wales, to the Duke of Roxburghe, thanking him for the present of two horses.

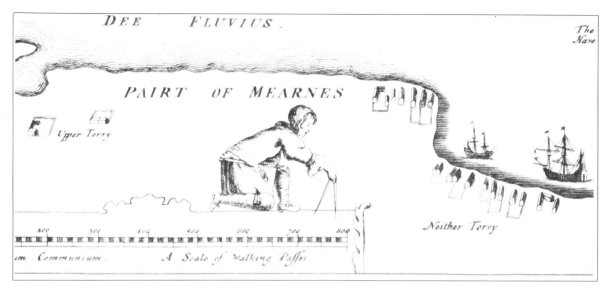

A detail from a map of Aberdeen by James Gordon, 1661. It was quite usual for maps to have illustrations on them, or to have a decorative border. Such illustrations give a good idea of life at the time. Here a kilted schoolboy kneels to use his compasses or dividers – as many children had to do when there was no furniture.

Farmers were often so poor themselves that they had no money for the teacher's salary and had to pay him in oatmeal instead. Often the poor schoolmaster had to trudge all round the parish to collect it.

There were no proper schools and classes met in barns and byres and old sheds. Sometimes the children lay on their stomachs and used the floor as a desk, and in other schools they took it in turn to sit at the table and benches. Even so, Scotland was ahead of the other countries of Europe in having a national school system at all and during the eighteenth century most lowland Scottish boys and girls learned to read and write.

Burgh schools flourished as Scotland's overseas trade increased and merchants wanted education for their sons. To become a member of a merchant guild a boy already had to serve a five-year apprenticeship in the arts of commerce and go overseas with a cargo at least three times.

Ships from Edinburgh, Dundee and Aberdeen traded regularly with Trondheim, Danzig, Rotterdam and Veere in the north and La Rochelle, Bordeaux and Spain in the south.

By 1690, however, Scottish merchants began to feel a grievance against their English neighbours. English merchants were growing rich through trade with their colonies in the West Indies and America but Scottish merchants were not allowed to trade there.

In 1695 they formed a trading company and tried to set up a colony of their own, at Darien, on the narrow strip of land between North and South America. Burgesses all over the lowlands invested money in the scheme and looked forward to new prosperity. It was a terrible shock when the scheme failed. Darien was unhealthy, the colonists were struck down by malaria, there was no sale for their goods and they were attacked by

SEVENTEENTH CENTURY: Schools

Gladstone's Land, an old merchant's house in Edinburgh's Lawnmarket. The booth (shop) would have been on ground level with the outside staircase leading to the house above.

The Merchants' House, Glasgow, headquarters of the Merchants' Guild, was founded in 1601 and rebuilt in 1659, a sign of the merchants' prosperity. Only the tower remains. A carving above the door is shown on page 77.

Spaniards. In 1700 they abandoned the colony, bitter because the English gave them no help.

Already there had been trouble in the highlands, where the MacDonalds had been massacred in 1692 on orders from the government at Westminster. It only needed another misfortune to make the Scots wish to break away from the union which had begun when James VI took the English crown.

The coat of arms of the company which wanted ▶ to establish a trading centre at Darien (Panama). The failure of the scheme hit all Scottish merchants very badly.

The second Duke of Queensberry (son of the builder of Drumlanrig Castle) worked very astutely to prepare the Act of Union 1707. Here he presents the Act to Queen Anne.

Gold unit (James VI) reverse on page 80.

Silver thirty-shilling piece (Charles I)

Silver two-merk piece (Charles II)

PRE-UNION COINS

Copper bawbee (William and Mary) with thistle reverse.

18 THE ACT OF UNION

Fresh disaster came between 1695 and 1702 with seven years of famine. The weather was so bad that farmers could not harvest until January or February. Summers brought nothing but rain, heavy frosts came down in early autumn and blizzards and deep snowdrifts followed in the winter.

In some parishes over one-third of the people died of hunger and others survived only by eating weeds, docks and wild spinach – and even snails. It was a time of 'blue faces and clean teeth' and landlords had no money to help their tenants.

Feeling against England ran so high that the English government feared that Scotland would break away and become a separate country under its own ruler. The Scots might even ally with England's enemy, France.

To stop this it suggested that Scotland should give up its Parliament and join with other parts of Britain with full rights to trade with England and her colonies. This big common market would help to build up Scottish prosperity. In 1707 the Act of Union joined the countries together.

Under the Act of Union Scotland gave

The Old Pretender, 'James VIII', father of ▶ Bonnie Prince Charlie, landing at Peterhead in January 1716 to encourage the ill-organised Jacobite Rebellion (the 'Fifteen') against George I.

up its Parliament at Edinburgh and agreed to send 45 Members to the House of Commons in London. Scottish lords chose 16 peers to represent them in the House of Lords.

Scotland kept its own laws and Presbyterian Church and its own system of education but coinage, weights and measures were to be common. A new flag, the Union Jack, was designed to include the cross of St. Andrew and the crosses of St. George and St. David.

It was some years before the Union began to bring real prosperity to the country, for at first the small Scottish industries could not compete with the large English trading companies. There were troubles also because the Jacobites wished to replace the German-born king George I by descendants of the House of Stewart.

In 1715 the Jacobites of Scotland and northern England began a rebellion to put James VII's son, James Stewart, on the throne as James VIII. Though it put down the rebellion easily enough the British government had to pay closer attention to what was happening in the distant north, where the clansmen still spoke their ancient Gaelic tongue and followed their own customs.

'The March of George I's Forces and Cannon to ▶ Perth' 1715. Moving the royal cannon northward took a long time – to judge from the number of horses yoked to the cannon and from the activity of the engineers clearing a road.

Kenneth Sutherland, Lord Duffus, in highland dress, about 1700. He wears a slashed doublet and linen shirt with a belted plaid which serves as 'kilt' and cloak combined.

Highlanders wearing the plaid in various ways: one part of the long strip of cloth forms a 'kilt', the rest is slung over one shoulder or pulled over both shoulders as a cloak.

19 Eighteenth Century: HIGHLANDS

The highland chiefs had lost some of their power in the seventeenth century but they were still the most important men in the north. Their clansmen revered them, and did their bidding without a murmur. Chiefs still ruled the countryside through their private law courts and in the wilder parts they still had power of life and death over their people.

Even in the eighteenth century chiefs were still warlords, and they counted their wealth in the number of fighting men they could call upon in time of need.

Many still encouraged their tenants to carry on the old sport of cattle lifting and took a share of the spoils. Some, like MacDonell of Barisdale, offered 'protection' from robbers: farmers paid 'blackmail' so that their cattle would not be stolen. MacDonell made £500 a year in this way.

Next in rank were the chief's relatives, *tacksmen*, who paid the chief a small rent for estates and then rented land out to the

An old droving route through the heart of the highlands. Animals had to be taken to market live – there was no means of transport.

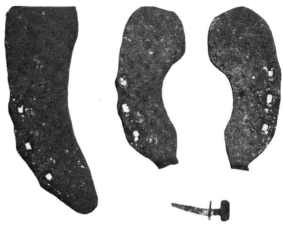

Cattle shoes were made for centuries. Those on the right were made by smiths in a Perthshire village about 1865.

Cattle being driven through the shallow waters of the Solway Firth.

lesser tenants and sub-tenants. Chiefs and tacksmen were the warleaders of the clan, owners of the biggest herds of black cattle.

Cattle-rearing was an important part of the highland way of life. Clansmen and chief alike depended on selling cattle at Trysts held at Crieff and elsewhere. The beasts were small (25–30 stone as against modern cattle averaging 64–88 stone) but hardy, and they cost nothing to transport. After the Trysts they were fitted with special shoes and driven south to the markets of England.

A visitor to Crieff in 1723 described the appearance of the chiefs and their followers, armed to the teeth:

> The highland gentlemen were mighty civil, dressed in their slashed waistcoats and trousing (which is breeches and stocking in one piece of striped stuff) with a plaid for a cloak and a blue bonnet. They have a poiniard, knife and fork in one sheath hanging at one side of their belt, their pistol at the other and their snuffmill before, with a great broadsword at their side. Their attendance was very numerous, all in belted plaids, girt like women's petticoats down to the knee, leaving thighs and half the leg all bare. They had also each a broadsword and a poiniard.

Field Marshal Lord George Wade 1673–1748. Here he is in armour but he usually wore the long coat and breeches shown on page 97. He earned more fame building roads and bridges than by fighting. The bridge, his finest, is over the Tay at Aberfeldy.

The Government in London was much alarmed by the Rebellion of 1715 and by tales of disorder, robbery, cattle rustling and blackmail that reached London. In 1724 it sent General Wade to Inverness as Commander-in-Chief, to keep the highlands quiet.

Wade quickly recruited six Highland Companies, to patrol the mountain passes and distant glens. Then he collected in illegal weapons from the clansmen and began to build roads. These were to link the garrisons at Fort William, Fort Augustus and Fort George (Inverness).

The road made a route now followed by the A82 and B852 and was finished in 1728. Wade then set 300 men to work on a road to Dunkeld.

Captains and lieutenants supervised the road building. Serjeants became foremen and privates provided the labour. Each day they worked on the road the officers got 2/6d, the serjeants and skilled tradesmen got 1/–d, corporals and drummers 8d, and privates 6d.

Letters written by Captain Burt, one of Wade's staff officers, are our best guide to highland life at the time.

Highland shielings on Jura: the shielings (rather like Indian wigwams covered in wattle) were used as temporary homes during the summer grazing season in upland pastures.

He was greatly surprised at the difference in appearance between chiefs and tacksmen, on the one hand, and the ordinary people. 'The gentry may be said to be a handsome people', he wrote, 'but the commonalty much otherwise; one would hardly think by their faces that they were the same species.'

The difference was due to bad food, exposure to weather and the everlasting reek of peat fires. In the long winters much time was spent sheltering from the weather and the smoke yellowed the skin and inflamed the eyes.

The poverty horrified the captain, when he saw the tiny amounts of goods brought for sale at the Inverness fair: a small roll of linen, a piece of plaiding, a pound or two of cheese or butter or a few goatskins.

The costume also worried him. He described the men as half naked, dressed in a large plaid girded to form a combined kilt and cloak. At least they wore brogues. Women went barefoot, in the coldest weather. In fishing towns he watched, amazed, as they carried their husbands ashore from the boats.

Women carry their husbands (with laden creels) from fishing boats in the early century.

The view that travellers saw as they approached Inverness from the south-west in the early eighteenth century. The castle was blown up by the Jacobite forces before the Battle of Culloden.

Inverness was the chief trading town of the north. Burt describes it as a town of 'four streets', a tiny place, and its shops and warehouses were poorly stocked.

Houses, as in other burghs along the Moray Firth, were built Dutch-style, with their backs to the street and a courtyard reached through an alleyway. Living quarters were reached by an outside stair, and the ground floor used as warehouse or shop. It was only in the great burghs that builders used properly squared stone. In Inverness and elsewhere houses were built of rubble and the walls made homes for thousands of rats, their nests hidden by the harling on the outside of the walls.

The gentry, bailies and shopkeepers all dressed English-style and spoke English as well as Gaelic or 'Irish', as Burt calls it. Gaelic was the only language spoken by most people in the north and west as far south as Loch Lomond.

Shopkeepers were well-off and could afford two or three maidservants. The poor girls were fed on oatmeal and paid three half crowns a year. Every moment of their 'spare' time was spent spinning for their mistress.

Captain Burt's journeys often took him on journeys beyond Inverness. He met highland chiefs with retinues of haunchman, piper, spokesman and numerous gillies – each gillie had a special task. One led the chief's horse over precipitous country, another looked after the baggage and another crossed before when the chief forded a flooded stream.

Burt describes one October journey in detail. He rode on horseback, a bag of lemons at the saddlebow for making brandy punch and a second horse carrying his portmanteau. His guide padded along on foot.

They crossed the first river on an ancient

Women sitting by a long trough sing as they felt home-woven cloth with their bare feet. A young man in bonnet and plaid leans on a staff — apparently doing nothing.

This picture of a mounted officer (detail from an engraving of the Battle of Culloden 1746) gives an idea of Captain Burt's appearance.

ferry boat sixty years old, patched with rough timber. The oars were held in place by the highlander's favourite twine, twisted birch roots.

The second obstacle was a peat bog, where the captain in his heavy boots broke through and the packhorse sank up to its neck.

He tackled another river by riding through it, practising the skill of fixing his eyes on the opposite bank and ignoring the rushing water. On another occasion he inched his way across two slender pine trees which formed a bridge and dragged the horse along by its reins.

Women grind corn, using a pivoted stick to rotate the quern (see pages 5 and 107).

Slezer at Kelso: horse ferry over the Tweed. Elsewhere, horses often had to swim rivers.

Flora Macdonald from South Uist was jailed for smuggling Prince Charles to Skye disguised as her maid. She later spent 30 years in America.

An imaginary picture of Charles with Antoine Walsh on the shore of Loch Nan Uamh, Inverness, having landed from a French ship, August 1745. In fact he usually wore trews.

At night they reached a small clachan and Burt went into the farmer's house while another hut was made ready for his night's stay.

The floor was soft earth with metre-high walls made of wattles packed on the outside with turf. A framework of naturally crooked timbers held up the heavy roof beam whose weight helped to stop the house being blown away during gales.

The wife and family of naked children squatted round a central peat fire. When Burt's eyes began to smart he went outside to dodge the smoke. He was amazed to see smoke pouring out of the roof, ribs and door of his own lodging, so that it looked like a steaming dung hill.

Once the newly lit peats had burned down to a steady glow, he found his quarters very comfortable. Sheets and blankets were spotlessly clean and, best of all, there were no bugs or fleas.

He could not eat the meat offered to him and, as usual, had boiled eggs instead.

Private, 92nd Gordon Highlanders 1815. When highland dress was later revived among civilians, it copied the military style.

EIGHTEENTH CENTURY: Highland lodging

A highland clachan at Loch Doich, Wester Ross, in 1880. Highland dwellings had changed little since the days when Captain Burt rode past in the early eighteenth century.

Like most visitors to the north, he found it hard to get used to highland cooking.

The Jacobites used Wade's roads in their dash for Edinburgh in 1745. The '45 was much less dangerous than it seemed, however. Many clan leaders had no wish for a Stewart on the throne and gave no help to Prince Charles Edward, 'Bonnie Prince Charlie'.

The clansmen who fought at Culloden followed their chiefs as heroically and devotedly as ever. Their defeat really marks the end of the old highland way of life all over the north and west. The government at once passed severe laws banning the kilt and bagpipe and the carrying of weapons. It also confiscated the lands of rebel chiefs and took them under government control, and put an end to the private law courts of all highland lords.

During the next thirty years government trustees spent the rents from the forfeited estates improving life for the highland people, building roads, bridges and

Burt stayed in houses like this during his travels. A pot hangs from the ceiling over a peat fire burning on a central hearth.

schools.

Chiefs encouraged young men to join the new Highland Regiments (they got £3 for every recruit) and highlanders fought Britain's wars in Europe and North America. The government in London was sure of highland loyalty by 1782. It ended the laws against highland dress and pipes and allowed the chiefs to return to their estates.

The Bear Gates at Traquair House, Peebles, built 1737–8. Four gallons of ale were provided for the workmen who erected them. According to one tradition, the 5th Earl of Traquair, a staunch Jacobite, closed the main gates in 1745 after saying farewell to Prince Charles and vowed that they would not be re-opened until the Stuart kings were restored to the throne. They are still kept closed today.

A concealed portrait of Prince Charles: the artist painted the features on the wooden base but they are visible as a recognisable face only in the reflection glass, when looked at from the right direction.

The thirty years of peace ended the old highland way of life. Chiefs no longer fostered sons out, to live among fellow clansmen, to learn Gaelic and to make friends among the people. They now hired lowland tutors or sent their sons south to learn English ways. When they grew up, landowners of the new generation thought highland customs ridiculous and did their best to change them. Chiefs who had spent thirty years in exile in Holland, France and Germany did not remember how their clansmen had suffered at Culloden. They were interested only in the income that their rents would bring.

The tacksmen found that they were no longer needed or respected. Chiefs did not need fighting men now and asked the tacksmen to pay higher rents. Many tacksmen were too proud to stay where they were no longer needed. They emigrated to America, sometimes taking their tenants with them and setting up clans of their own in the New World.

People found it harder to pay higher rents, for the population grew rapidly in the late eighteenth century and farms became smaller with each new generation.

Already many people had left the islands and highlands, driven out by starvation. Hundreds of poor people in Skye lived just like the *strand loopers* of the Middle Stone Age, eating little except limpets and shell-fish.

Thousands of highlanders moved to the lowland towns in search of work and others emigrated to North Carolina and Canada.

Many highland families were saved from starvation by growing potatoes which became their main food supply. To pay

A twentieth-century photograph of one of the oldest thatched cottages on South Uist. They still rely on heavy stones to hold on the thatch, but modern wire netting is more effective than ropes.

'Town Guard' by David Allan (1744–1796). Many guards were highlanders, taking work in towns.

Grinding corn in Skye in the nineteenth century by the old method.

their rents and buy necessities they could not grow on the farm – iron tools, leather, salt and needles – they depended on selling cattle to the drovers who toured the glens each year. Fresh meat was needed for English towns and to supply the navy with salt beef. Britain was at war with either France or Spain for most of the eighteenth century and the Napoleonic Wars lasted till 1815.

Landowners with a quick eye for profit soon realised that sheep, which supplied both wool and meat, brought bigger profits than cattle. Sheep could also survive better on the short grass of hillsides.

In 1762 the graziers from the Borders rented pastures in Argyll, Dumbartonshire and Perthshire; and soon looked for more land in Ross-shire and Sutherland.

EIGHTEENTH CENTURY: Highland sheep farms

This drawing records a common sight of the early nineteenth century, a ship waiting for for highland families forced to emigrate because they had been evicted from their crofts.

Left : black-faced highland sheep have curling horns and long coarse fleece. They are hardy, good mutton and providers of excellent wool for tweed manufacture. Right : great Cheviot sheep 'ate up' the highlands. White-faced, hornless, they provide a medium-weight wool free from dark streaks. Heads and upper legs have no thick wool.

Sheep-farming brought disaster to the highland peasants. There was no room on the hillsides for black cattle and soft-fleeced highland sheep once the herds of big white Cheviot and Black Face Linton sheep arrived. As the sheep moved in the people had to move out.

Others left because they were driven out when their old chiefs, the landowners, decided to rent out the land for sheep grazing. Sheep farmers could pay twenty times more rent than the peasant farmers. Landowners gave their tenants notice to quit, tore down houses and farm build-ings and turned farms into pasture.

These 'Clearances' brought great sadness and bitterness. People did not wish to leave the glens where their ancestors had lived for centuries. One of the worst Clearances took place in Sutherland where 15 000 people were turned off.

People who did not move quickly enough were brutally driven out, as in Strathnaver (Sutherland) in 1819. The factor offered them land on the coast, so that they could set up as fishermen, but they had no boats, no money and no experience. It was a miserable exchange.

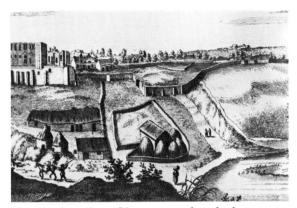

At Dunfermline, Slezer saw thatched cottages, barns and conical haystacks enclosed by a neat wall – probably built of stones from the old abbey. Transport is the same as on page 84.

Wide unfenced fields near Arbroath. The farm-workers are followed by a man with a horse and sled. Sledges were in common use because trackways were too rough for cart wheels.

20 Eighteenth Century: LOWLANDS

When Daniel Defoe visited Scotland after the Union he found it foreign in every way. In his 'Tour of Great Britain' he described how the moment he crossed the Border an icy 'Scots gale' made him cover his eyes and dismount from his horse, in case he was blown off.

He marvelled at the bleak wastes of Coldingham Moor and the lack of trees. Even the food was different. The herrings at Dunbar were red in colour, cured differently from those of Yarmouth and he found one delicacy, a Soland goose, impossible to eat because it tasted of fish. (A Soland 'goose' is a gannet.)

Sometimes he admired what he saw, but he thought farming methods were backward and the soil impoverished. The tenanted farms were still divided into rigs and worked jointly by the tenants and cottars of the farm-touns. The poorest cottars struggled to keep alive by working as paid labourers and by growing oats on a small patch of ground.

Scottish landowners who journeyed to England also saw differences between the two countries. In particular they looked at the prosperous English farms and decided to change matters at home.

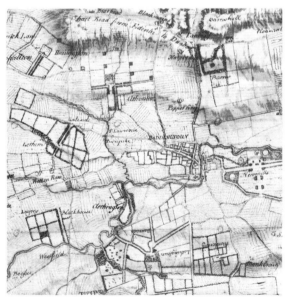

On Roy's map of East Lothian (1750s) some rigs are shown already enclosed to make farms that landlords could rent to single tenants.

Men digging in a field near Glasgow. The tree-lined road later became Argyle Street. The view includes the Cathedral on the left and Bishop Rae's Old Bridge on the right.

Already at the end of the seventeenth century wealthy landowners were planting trees in their own parklands, as Slezer shows in this view of Argile House.

Portobello, near Edinburgh, was a village that grew up because of fine clay deposits, used for bricks and for white stoneware. Coloured figurines and pots were prized possessions.

Their improvements were to change the look of the Scottish countryside. They enclosed fields with hedges and ditches and planted new crops, clover and turnips, to enrich the soil and to provide feed for cattle in the winter. They also encouraged farmers to follow the English pattern of growing turnips, peas, oats and clover in turn.

Above all they planted trees. Most of the plantations, copses and woods of today were started by the tree-planting landowners. The Earl of Loudon planted a million trees in Ayrshire, the Earl of Stair planted 20 000 trees a year in Wigtown. The Earl of Atholl planted new sorts of trees as well as old, millions of fir, oak, elm, ash, walnut, beech, laburnum as well as larch trees which he brought in from the Tyrol in Austria.

The improved farms brought more profits to the landlords and better food to the tenants. Potatoes, turnips and sometimes beef or mutton helped out their old diet.

With more money available tea-drinking became popular. Some people thought that tea-drinking was bad for the health and others advised that a little whisky was

Teaset c. 1790 in the Dumfries Burgh Museum. Tea drinking came from China – and Chinese teacups today are often made without handles.

needed in the last cup to cancel out the bad effects of the tea. Old-fashioned ministers preached against both tea and whisky as equally bad for the drinker. In the towns, bakers began to specialise in the tea-breads and pastries that go so well with tea-drinking.

Other signs of prosperity appeared in farmers' houses at the end of the century. Ministers who wrote about their parishes for the first Statistical Account of 1790 describe how nearly ever farmer's house now had an eight-day clock and every farm servant a watch. These were still very precious possessions, carefully handed down from father to eldest son.

A grandfather clock made in Dumfries 1745. The mechanism is worked by weights and a pendulum inside the tall case. The clockfaces of such clocks were decorated in various ways, some being gilded and others painted in different colours to show scenes of country life.

Woodhead Farm: an early eighteenth-century lowland farm, home of the Baird family of Gartsherrie.

High Cross Farm to which the Bairds moved in 1808. The new house is tiled, not thatched, and the walls are built of dressed stone.

An Edinburgh fishwife from Kay's 'Original Portraits' 1792. She wears a spotted muslin headscarf and boldly striped skirts. Her basket is full of oysters for selling in the streets or at houses.

Ministers noticed a great difference in costume, also, when people came to the kirk in their best clothes. The Cambuslang Minister wrote:

> When a farmer's family went to the kirk (in 1750) he and his sons wore suits of home-made cloth, plaidin hose and blue or black bonnets; his wife and daughters were dressed in gowns of their own spinning, both cloaks and hoods, worsted stockings and leather shoes.

By 1790 things had changed:

> He and his sons wore suits of English cloth, worsted or cotton stockings and hats; his wife and daughters were dressed in printed calico or silk gowns, scarlet wool or silk cloaks, silk bonnets, white thread stockings and cloth shoes.

Other writers, including Robert Burns (1759–94), tell us of the finery worn by young ploughmen and farmers, plush or corduroy breeches, long broadcloth coats, velvet waistcoats, fine linen shirts with ruffled fronts, fringed muslin cravats and black silk shoulder knots. Women wore gay muslins, silks and printed cottons.

These descriptions show that many country people were better-off and that there were new goods to buy, textiles

This view of a cottage interior, by David Allan, says a great deal about cooking, costume, customs and manners, furnishings and toys. Allan drew many scenes of social life.

made in mills in Scotland as well as in England.

The people who wore this finery still lived in the roughest houses. Good building materials (dressed stone, seasoned timber, laths, planking, slates and plaster) were too expensive and too difficult to transport.

In some parts, such as East Lothian, the soil was richer and the tenant farmers more prosperous and their houses roomier and more comfortable. The house area was about the same, but the barn at one end and the byre and stable at the other were separate buildings with their own entrances.

The farmhouse was divided into two rooms, the but and the ben. The but was the main living room, used as kitchen, dining room, sitting room and bedroom for the grown-up daughters and female servants. The ben was a better room, sometimes with a wooden floor instead of beaten earth, and the farmer, his wife and the young children used it as their sleeping place.

The sons slept upstairs in the garrets, rooms made by laying floorboards across the ceiling joists and lit by little windows cut in the gable-ends. Male farm servants slept on a platform built over the horses' heads in the stable.

Farmhouses like this had chimneys cut into the gables and in the but wooden settles were set in the inglenook to make a cosy place to sit in the evening.

Rural household utensils in the eighteenth century. Top row, left to right: wrought iron toaster, baking stone. Bottom, left to right: bread spade, girdle, bannock spade.

Left to right: bowl, luggie — with two horn spoons.

In these houses the walls were higher, about 2 metres, and plastered, while the small windows were filled with diamond-shaped panes of glass set in lead. Kitchen utensils were different, too. By the end of the century a farmer's wife could buy cast-iron pots, kettles and pails which were cheaper and longer-lasting than those made of copper or wood.

All these houses were luxurious compared with those of the poor cottars. They lived in hovels made of rough stones or turf about 4 metres square, with a smoke-hole in the divot roof and one glass-less window protected by a wooden shutter.

Even as late as 1871 a third of country dwellers reared families of eight or more in single-roomed houses, while about another third never had more than two rooms.

Both in town and country it was hard to get away from dirt and smell. Human and animal manure was piled up in a great heap in the courtyard before the farm-house, and visitors wisely kept to the causeway of flat stones that led up to the house door. If they stepped off they might easily sink up to the knee in foul smelling mud and water.

Countryfolk forgot the hard-working day at the local fair. Dressed in their best, they gaped at the wandering jugglers, acrobats and candy-sellers. Old people gossiped, young people flirted and, according to the ministers, they all took far too much whisky, snuff and tobacco.

Communion time brought crowds of people together from villages and farm-touns to listen to open-air sermons. They found time at these 'Holy Fairs' for merry-making as well.

At Hallowe'en and Hogmanay they still celebrated the old pagan feasts, partly for the fun of it and also because many people still believed in witches and fairies and magic. Burns' poem about a Hallowe'en describes how the young people, half in terror, tried to foresee who their future wives and husbands would be like. One way was to peep into a mirror, and another was to pull up a cabbage stump.

Christenings, funerals and marriages were social occasions, also. The Penny Weddings were cheerful affairs. All the guests contributed food and drink for the feast; in earlier days the gift was a penny.

Bride and groom lead off the dance in David Allan's 'Penny Wedding'. The company below make merry and young spectators look down from the loft. Garrets in a farmhouse were usually built in this style.

Most activities changed slowly over the centuries before the invention of steam-driven machinery. This picture of Glasgow Fair was drawn in 1825. It includes the same kinds of entertainment as those of the Middle Ages – though costume has changed.

David Allan's 'Highland Dance' shows dancing in the open air to the music of strings and bagpipes. The highland costume is already changing from that shown on page 73.

The inn scene at the beginning of 'Tam o'Shanter', the famous poem by Robert Burns. Tam sits drinking in the inglenook by a blazing fire with the landlord and landlady and his crony Souter Johnny. When he leaves the inn, full of drink, Tam is chased by witches and warlocks whom he disturbs in Alloway Kirk.

Men gathered at country inns, such as the famous inn where Tam o'Shanter tarried too long and nearly got carried off by the devil.

Women had their own special gatherings, the 'Rockings'. Every little farmhouse made its own yarn for weaving and unmarried girls spent so much time spinning that the name 'spinster' is still used today.

Spinning took up all the spare minutes between farm and household tasks, as well as evening hours. Often the girls took their distaffs and spindles to a barn or cottage and did their spinning in company, gossiping and 'spinning yarns'. These meetings were known as 'rockings' after the 'rocks' or spindles used by the women.

Sometimes the young men came along, too, and there would be dancing, and so the distaffs and spindles, or 'rocks' and 'reels' gave their names to Scottish dances.

Rev. Robert Walker by Henry Raeburn of Edinburgh. Skating was a traditional sport.

A girl spinning with distaff and spindle (p. 56).

A cartoon picture of David Dale.

When the linen industry and then the cotton industry became important in Scotland manufacturers found plenty of skilled spinners and weavers who could handle the new fine yarns.

Many Scottish merchants hoped to sell great supplies of linen in England after the Union but they had no success. Scottish flax was poor and the finished linen was coarse and yellow. Most trade and industry in Scotland did badly and the Parliament at Westminster set up a special Board of Commissioners to find ways of helping them. The Board spent its money wisely, giving money to flax growers, bringing in expert spinners and weavers from Flanders and France, and setting up Spinning Schools where more girls could learn to use spinning wheels.

After 1727 the linen trade began to flourish, especially in Forfar and Fife, which specialised in making coarser cloths, and in Lanarkshire and Renfrewshire, which concentrated on the finer

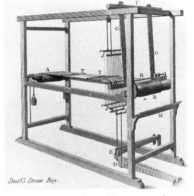

The type of handloom used before power-driven looms made factory-produced cloth cheaper.

cloth needed for handkerchiefs, neckerchiefs and dress materials. Linen goods were printed in gay stripes and checks and the brightly striped headscarves popular with women became known as 'Glasgows'.

Linen merchants often became rich. The most famous was David Dale, who served his time as a weaver in Paisley and then opened a shop in Glasgow High Street in 1761.

View of Glasgow 1764 by Robert Paul. The tower of the Merchants' House (see page 95) is second from the right. Towers from left to right: Hutcheson's Hospital – then in Argyle Street (see Heriot's School on page 87), Old Ramshorn Church, Glasgow Cathedral, University (the Old College), Tron Church, the Tolbooth, Merchants' House and St. Andrews Church.

His business was very successful. He imported fine yarn from Flanders and had it woven by local weavers. By 1794 he was interested in the idea of using cotton instead of linen. Cotton cloth was cheaper, softer and finer. One manufacturer, James Menteith, set up a whole village of cotton weavers in Anderston, a village which then lay just outside Glasgow.

Helped by Richard Arkwright, inventor of the Water Frame, Dale chose a site for his mill by the Falls of Clyde near Lanark. Here the fast-flowing water was harnessed to drive spinning machines.

Work in the cotton mills called for quick fingers rather than great strength. Women and children made the best workers, for they were biddable and cheap to employ.

The mills were huge by eighteenth-century standards. In 1795 Dale employed 1334 workers. He had to provide homes for these workpeople. He built long rows of tenements in the narrow valley by the mills, and called his settlement New Lanark.

Dale was a very religious man and highly interested in education, so the apprentices attended school from 7.30 to 9 p.m. The school also catered for the children of the village so that 570 children attended the school, which was taught by sixteen teachers. It was open on Sundays for those who could not squeeze into the kirk and for religious education in the afternoon. There was no work on Sundays.

Among those employed were 398 orphan children taken from the poor houses of Edinburgh and Glasgow. Dale got good value from these 'apprentices' who received no wages but were kept, clothed and fed until the age of fifteen.

Visitors thought he treated his child workers very well. The working day lasted $11\frac{1}{2}$ hours, from 6 a.m. to 7 p.m. with half an hour off for breakfast at nine and an hour's break for dinner at two.

Food was plentiful. The children could eat as much bread as they wanted before starting work, and for breakfast and supper they had porridge and milk. For dinner they ate broth with potatoes and bread, with meat one day and cheese on the next.

EIGHTEENTH CENTURY: Cotton

Above : Corra Linn in 1812. The Falls of Clyde have today lost much of their splendour through being harnessed for hydro-electric power, except when the sluices are opened.   Below : David Dale's model village of New Lanark is crammed into the narrow steep-sided valley of the Clyde. The mills no longer work but the rows of houses have been renovated into modern flats.

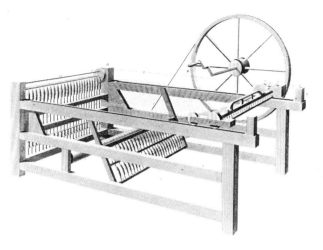

A hand-spinner, using a spinning wheel, could spin thread on to one spool at a time. Using the Spinning Jenny (invented by James Hargreaves in 1765) the spinner could feed thread on to as many as 100 spindles at once.

A lowland foot soldier of the regiment later called the King's Own Scottish Borderers. The unusual plant in the foreground records the regiment's service in Minorca 1769–1775.

The factory children wore cotton clothes in summer and linen dresses or woollen suits in the winter. As was common in eighteenth-century Scotland they went barefoot in the summer months.

At night they slept in six large dormitories, three to a bed, with proper sheets and blankets. Dale paid a great deal of attention to health and hygiene. Dormitories were scrubbed every week and whitewashed once a year. The children's clothes were washed every fortnight.

When they reached the age of fifteen the apprentices were dismissed since they would now have to be paid. Girls usually went into domestic service and became maidservants in the houses of the gentry. Boys joined the army, became apprentice joiners, carpenters or, very often, weavers.

Dale and other manufacturers built big water-driven mills at Catrine, Blantyre, Dean, Balfron, Stanley and other places but most weaving still had to be done on hand looms until the 1820s; there was a great deal of home spinning, too. By 1800 there were 82 000 people working in the cotton industry, in mills, at home or as part-time workers.

One of the most unusual and remarkable men to come from the farming and weaving villages of west Scotland was Robert Burns whose poems were published in Kilmarnock in 1786. They stunned the literary clubs in Edinburgh who found it hard to believe that an Ayrshire farmer would have anything to write or even be able to write it.

Burns really owed little to the parish school, for he lived too far away. His father, a devout and religious man, persuaded his neighbours to join in paying a young student named John Murdoch to come and teach grammar, writing, arithmetic and psalm-singing to their children. Murdoch was paid sixpence a day and taught them for two years, till Burns was nine and had to start full-time work on the farm.

Before his poems appeared in print, Robert Burns had decided to emigrate. His father had died of overwork and disappointment as one farm after another failed to give him a decent living. Now Burns found himself a successful poet,

Portrait of Robert Burns by Alexander Nasmyth. Both believed that people are of equal worth, regardless of wealth or rank. So Nasmyth could get no more portrait work from the rich.

invited to the fashionable city of Edinburgh to meet the cream of Scottish society.

A shoemaker at work drawn by C. Smith about 1810.

David Allan's 'Fireman' does not seem well equipped to deal with the fire.

Edinburgh chimney sweeps : ladder, brush and sack.

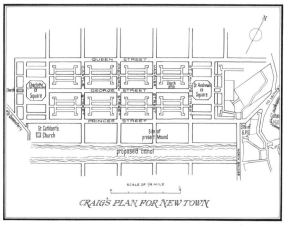

Edinburgh New Town was built to Craig's plan but the proposal for a canal was abandoned. The modern aerial view is from the west.

21 Eighteenth Century: CITY LIFE

Eighteenth-century Edinburgh attracted people from all parts of Scotland, ministers to the General Assembly, wealthy merchants to the Convention of Royal Burghs and nobles and country gentlemen to their town houses.

Above all, Edinburgh was the place where the chief Law Court met, the Court of Session. Many Edinburgh lawyers became wealthy men and bought up country estates.

As the Old Town became more crowded richer people began to look for more elegant and spacious houses out of the smell and stir of the packed closes and narrow streets. The Lord Provost, George Drummond, found the answer: he planned a New Town to be built on re-claimed swamp land by the Nor'Loch. The Town Council invited architects to enter a competition to find the best plan and in 1762 it was won by a 27-year-old architect named James Craig.

He suggested a grid-iron pattern. Three long wide thoroughfares, George Street, Queen Street and Princes Street were linked by cross streets and at each end of George Street there was a handsome square. Many of the elegant houses were designed by the great Scots architect Robert Adam.

With the development of the New Town, Edinburgh flourished as a centre of arts and fashion.

It had the first licensed theatre in Scotland, opened in 1762 in spite of the disapproval of the Kirk.

Another fashionable meeting-place was the Assembly Rooms, where ladies and gentlemen gathered to dance stately minuets and quadrilles. The dances were very formal affairs, the ladies in hooped skirts of velvet or silk, their hair piled high over wire cages, powdered and decorated, and the gentlemen in wigs, long tight-waisted coats, embroidered

Bewigged ministers and other gentlemen listen to a discussion in the General Assembly of the Kirk, the only national assembly in Scotland since 1707.

A view of Edinburgh in 1817, showing the 'Mound', built on rubbish piled in the middle of the Nor' Loch to link Princes Street with the High Street. Gardens now fill the hollow.

This Leith oyster cellar, depicted by Burnett, does not look as if it were meant for high society.

The ladies' hairstyles and dresses of 1800 were better for dancing than earlier fashions.

'The Painter's Wife' by Allan Ramsay, son of the Edinburgh poet and bookseller. The painter, born in 1713, was a highly educated and cultured man. He had studied in Rome and spoke several languages.

waistcoats, tight breeches and swords.

If they wanted more lively dancing they could join the merrier set who gathered in the oyster cellars to drink portar, eat oysters and dance Scottish reels.

Music lovers could attend performances of Handel and Mozart at the meetings of the Musical Society at St. Cecilia's Hall. Those interested in literature joined Scotland's first lending library, in Allan Ramsay's shop near the Mercat Cross. Here they met people with similar tastes and, after the fashion of the day, they formed clubs and societies.

This view from the south side of the Clyde in Glasgow. The bridge is the Broomielaw (Jamaica Street bridge) built 1763–1768 as Glasgow's second bridge and known as the 'Bonnie Brig' because of the decorative circles above each pier. The costume indicates that the drawing was made about 1800. The bridge was rebuilt 1832–1835. The smoking conical building on the left is the glassworks.

A wooden tobacco sign in the form of a Red Indian. By 1740 Glasgow merchants handled over half the American tobacco crop through their warehouses – most of it being exported to France. This and other forms of trade made Glasgow the chief shipping and commercial town of Scotland.

While Edinburgh thrived as the centre of fashion and high culture, Glasgow became the chief city of business. With the Union came the chance to build up trade with the North American colonies. Its merchants made great fortunes in sugar, rum and tobacco, and controlled most of the supply of tobacco to Europe. The American planters had to send all their tobacco to Britain first.

The tobacco trade slumped after the American War of Independence when planters could sell direct to other European countries. The cotton trade took its place. The Clyde was deepened so that ocean-going ships could come right up to the Broomielaw and in 1790 the city was linked to the east coast by the Forth-Clyde Canal.

In the middle of the century Glasgow was still a small town, with its merchants meeting at the Cross and carrying out their business on the plain stones, but thirty years later they met in the Chamber

Merchants meet by King William's statue in front of their Tontine Hotel (over the arcade) and the Tolbooth (guarded by a sentrybox). The plainstones (the only paving in the city) are fenced off. The Tontine Hotel was used as coffee house, assembly room and club.

A bank note from one of Glasgow's earliest banks, the Ship Bank. Notes were sometimes hard to change as small coins were often scarce.

of Commerce, founded in 1782 by Patrick Colquhoun, Provost of Glasgow.

As in Edinburgh, the wealthier citizens moved out into new suburbs, to George Square or Blythswood, or to the village of Gorbals on the south side of the river. Their old flats and tenements quickly filled up with people who flocked to work in Glasgow. The city's population shot up to 83 700 in 1801.

Glasgow could not match Edinburgh as a social centre, but its old university had some remarkable and world-famous professors, including Adam Smith and John Anderson. Smith was an economist whose book *The Wealth of Nations* was widely read by statesmen and businessmen. John Anderson is famous as the scientist who encouraged the inventor James Watt and began evening classes for adults at the Andersonian Institute. This was the first technical college in Europe and eventually became (1966) the University of Strathclyde.

Glasgow merchants were well-educated men, interested in literature and the arts, and they formed clubs on the Edinburgh pattern.

An open-air exhibition of paintings in the courtyard of the old Glasgow University in 1761.

A country inn yard showing passengers mounting a very clumsy-looking windowless coach with enormous wheels. Two men sprawl on the roof top and an old woman sits in the basket used for luggage. Later coaches had rails for the outside passengers to hang on to, and the basket gave way to a boot.

22 THE TRANSPORT REVOLUTION

The old trackways could not stand up to the needs of eighteenth-century merchants and travellers. Wheels sank deep into the mud and axles shattered as the vehicles bounced among ruts and stones.

Even Wade's gravel-surfaced roads could not stand up to wheeled traffic. When Lord Lovat drove from Inverness to Edinburgh in 1740 he took eleven days. The coach's rear axle broke twice and the front axle once. At times he got squads of men to drag the coach to the nearest black-

smith while his daughters perched unhappily behind the postilions on saddleless horses.

Waggoners tried to carry heavy goods by fitting enormous broad-rimmed wheels and harnessing large teams of horses.

Wealthy passengers could hire a postchaise and do the journey to London in six days, with luck.

Turnpike Roads were built by local landowners who clubbed together to lay new roads. They got their money back by

Thomas Telford, the great engineer, built fishing ports, canals and highways (including 1200 bridges) in all parts of the country.

making travellers pay tolls every few miles along the road. The names Tollcross, Allander Toll, and dozens of similar names tell us where these toll gates used to be.

Improved roads meant faster traffic. In 1766 a fast 'Fly' coach carried four passengers between Edinburgh and Glasgow in nine hours. Soon there were regular stage coach services between Edinburgh and the towns of Glasgow, Stirling and Perth.

The wheels of a two-ton coach travelling at 13 km/h tore up the road surfaces very quickly but John Loudon Macadam, an Ayrshire landowner, solved the problem when he laid his first new road between Ayr and Maybole in 1787.

The road was dug out to a depth of about 30 cm and filled with very small stones which became packed tight under the wheels of carts and carriages. Modern 'tar macadam' roads use this idea though the stones are now bound with tar to give a firmer surface.

Coach travel was a painful business. Inside passengers were terribly cramped on the narrow seats with knees nearly touching those of the person opposite. The outside passengers, perched more than 3 metres above the ground, had only a narrow rail to cling to. Whole coaches were sometimes buried in deep drifts on places like Fenwick Moor.

The postilion pays the toll-keeper his fee for letting a post chaise pass. The passenger inside looks rather nervous; perhaps she is worried about the luggage balanced on the roof. Averaging 18 km/h, a fast chaise could bring important news from London in 33 hours.

Ostlers steady the lively horses as the Glasgow mail coach prepares to leave the 'Bull and Mouth' inn, London, while a spectator looks down from one of the galleries that connect the upper rooms.

In 1784 the Post Office began a mail coach service covering the whole of Britain.

Mail coaches carried only a few passengers, some inside and some out, as well as driver and guard. The stage coaches run by private companies carried as many as 15 passengers.

Smartly painted, upper panels a glossy black, lower panels a deep maroon with gilded coats-of-arms, and wheels post-office red, the mail coaches brought a new idea of regularity and punctuality into eighteenth century life.

Operating the mails was big business and the Post Office insisted on perfect time-keeping. The guard's most important equipment, apart from his blunderbuss, horse pistols and horn, was his sealed watch, carried in a padlocked glass fronted box. Postmasters checked the mail coaches' time at each stop.

By 1830 the speed of the mail coaches was set at 16 km/h. It was a killing pace for horses. They had to be changed every 16 km. There were 40 stages on the Edinburgh–London run and to keep mail and stage coaches operating, thousands of horses were needed.

The speed and safety of the mail was the main consideration. When the mail coach stuck in heavy snow drifts by the Devil's Beef Tub near Moffat, driver and guard tried to ride the horses through on their

The old 'Saracen's Head', built in the Gallow-gate, Glasgow in 1754, with stones taken from the old Bishop's Castle, was the chief coaching station for many years, with stables for sixty horses. The first London–Glasgow mail coach reached it on 7 July 1788.

The guard carried a special watch, in a padlocked brass case in a pouch suspended from his shoulder. The postmaster used it to write in the time of the coach's departure. He also entered the time according to the local clocks or even sundials.

A sleepy gatekeeper at Stamford Hill turnpike lets the Edinburgh mail coach through on the last moonlit stage of the journey to London. The journey had been cut from seventy-eight hours in 1784 to forty-two in 1820.

own. Then they struggled through the blizzard on foot until they died of exposure, leaving the precious mail firmly fastened to a stout post.

The arrival of the mail was enormously exciting. Glasgow businessmen waited at their special clubroom, the Tontine Coffee House, for the blare of the guard's horn and the blunderbuss shot which announced the mail was ready.

When the mail coach brought news of a great victory such as Trafalgar (1805) the horses were wreathed in laurels, the guard wore his best gold-laced hat and scarlet coat and a red flag fluttered from the coach roof.

Glasgow businessmen waited eagerly for the mail and the newspapers. When the papers came there was a wild scramble as the waiter, Charles Gordon, threw the whole lot up into the air. Dignified lawyers and insurance men joined in this game with gusto until the day one gentleman had his teeth knocked out.

A stage coach 'The Bruce' passes two other coaches stuck in snowdrifts in the 1830s. Outside passengers need their triple-caped coats.

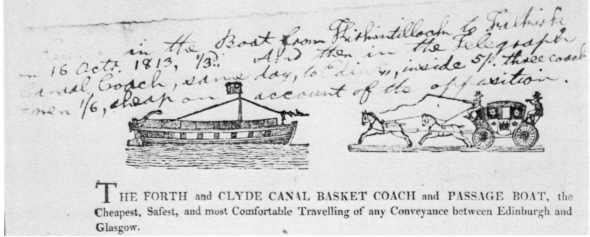

in the Boat from Kirkintilloch to Falkirk
16 Oct. 1813, 1/3.. And then in the Telegraph
Canal Coach, same day, to Edin. inside 5/. three coach
men 1/6, cheap on account of the opposition.

THE FORTH and CLYDE CANAL BASKET COACH and PASSAGE BOAT, the
Cheapest, Safest, and most Comfortable Travelling of any Conveyance between Edinburgh and
Glasgow.

This 1813 handbill advertises a new means of travelling between Glasgow and Edinburgh, and a passenger records his journey by boat and 'Telegraph'. Coaches often carried names to advertise their speed: 'Express', 'Tallyho', 'New Times'.

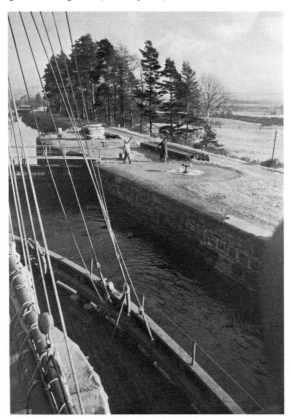

A fishing boat passes through one of the locks on the Caledonian Canal. Telford's great canal never became an important waterway. Fishing and tourist boats are the main traffic.

When bulk transport was needed to shift heavy loads of coal, ore and manufactured goods the Scots followed the English example of cutting canals. The Monkland Canal to link Lanarkshire mines with Glasgow and the Forth–Clyde Canal linking east and west were completed in 1790.

Other canals were built later, the Crinan Canal in 1801, the Inverurie–Aberdeen Canal in 1807, the Union Canal between Edinburgh and Falkirk and the huge Caledonian Canal in 1822.

Linked with stage coach services the canals provided a wonderfully fast service for passengers. The fastest and smoothest ride was on the Glasgow–Paisley Canal, where William Houston harnessed coach horses to a special barge. The light iron hull was 21·2 metres long, 1·7 metres wide and drew only 40 cm of water. It could hold 90 passengers and two fast horses, frequently changed, pulled it along at 19 km/h. Twelve boats operated daily between Glasgow and Paisley, carrying 423 186 passengers in 1836.

1760–1840: Canal transport

Excited crowds watched the opening of the Glasgow–Garnkirk railway on 27 September 1831. Most of the passengers were in open trucks and were astounded at the speed (about $7\frac{1}{2}$ mph).

In 1802 the first successful steamboat, the Charlotte Dundas, was used to pull barges across country from the Forth to Port Dundas.

The coming of steam put both coaches and canals out of business. The first steam trains ran on the Glasgow–Garnkirk and the Edinburgh–Dalkeith lines in 1831, and the Dundee–Newtyle line in 1832. After 1840 railway lines began to link the lowland towns and penetrate northwards, from Edinburgh to Perth and Dundee in 1847 and Inverness in 1863.

Railways joined England and Scotland more closely together. The Edinburgh–Berwick line was completed in 1846 and the Glasgow–Carlisle line in 1848.

The effects of rail transport were soon felt by all classes of people all over the country for, by law, the railway companies had to provide cheap transport and passengers could travel first, second or third class. Mail was speeded up (the 'penny post' came in 1840) and businessmen, workers and tourists travelled in comfort.

William Symington's 'sternwheeler', the 'Charlotte Dundas', proved the value of steam when it towed two laden sloops 19 miles in six hours against strong head winds, on the Forth–Clyde canal in 1802.

23 Nineteenth Century: MACHINES

Watt's double-acting rotative steam engine. James Watt of Greenock (1736–1819) improved the older atmospheric engine by fitting a condenser. He also adapted the engine to drive machinery. Steam power gradually replaced wind, water and muscle power in industry. For his own use, Watt designed this little stove with three covers to fit the top: a lid with chimney (while fire is drawing), a kettle and a lidded pan.

A nineteenth-century steam engine used to drive a threshing machine, one of the first steps in replacing human and animal muscle power on the farm.

132

NINETEENTH CENTURY: Agricultural change

The railways affected life in the country, too. Already landlords had realised that they could make great profits by supplying towns with food and they now rented out their land to farmers who could pay the highest rents. The new farms were solid blocks of land rented to one man and so the old farm-towns and separate rigs vanished.

The farmers soon made use of new Scottish inventions, James Small's swing-plough, Patrick Bell's reaper and Andrew Meikle's threshing machine. Farmers in the Lothians were the first to harness steam engines to drive the threshers. Unwanted farm labourers drifted into the towns.

Scientific farming methods made farmers well-to-do. They could now afford to build roomy stone houses, with three rooms downstairs and three or more upstairs. They furnished them better than the gentry had done in the eighteenth century, with mahogany furniture, carpets and even pianos. Scots farming became famous for efficiency.

New industries and transport services brought new kinds of work for ordinary people. Much of it was hard and monotonous and in the industrial areas working and living conditions were dangerously unhealthy. Neither Parliament nor the Town Councils realised how great the changes were.

Scotland had its first great ironworks at Carron, begun in 1769 and especially famous for its naval guns. Now the centre of iron manufacture swung over to Airdrie, Coatbridge and Motherwell after David Mushett found deposits of Blackband Ironstone in Lanarkshire in 1801.

This mixture of coal and iron was not easy to smelt until John Neilson suggested that hot air should be blasted into the furnaces instead of cold. The method was so successful that Scotland became the world's second largest iron producer, next in size to England.

The need for coal and iron expanded rapidly with the use of steam engines for all sorts of purposes. James Watt had adapted his engine to drive mill machinery in 1781, William Symington used it in a steam boat in 1788 and William Murdoch invented a steam locomotive in 1784.

Adam Smith explained that a nation's wealth was its people, working at producing goods for sale. Manufacturers could create a rich nation by using their profits to make more goods and to provide more jobs.

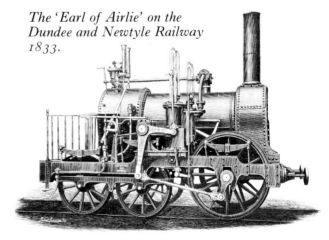

The 'Earl of Airlie' on the Dundee and Newtyle Railway 1833.

Two pictures from the report of the Royal Commission on the Mines 1842. Left : a girl carrying coal (Janet Cumming, 11 years old : I carry the large bits of coal from wall-face to pit bottom . . . the weight is usually a hundredweight.) Right : children being drawn up the mine shaft. There is no cage so they hang on as well as they can to the winding rope.

Coal mining had begun in the twelfth century. Until 1799 miners were little better than serfs. They often pledged that their children would serve in the mine all their lives, in return for an *arles*, a gift made by the mine owner at the time of the christening.

Sometimes criminals had been handed over as slaves, like Alexander Stewart, convicted of theft in Perth in 1701. He was sentenced to death, for there were over two hundred crimes for which people could be hanged in those days. Instead, he was granted to Sir John Erskine of Alva, to work as Sir John's 'perpetual servant'.

Miners worked under horrible conditions, even though they were free in the nineteenth century. They usually worked in family teams. Men hewed the coal, helped by the older boys who, according to age and strength, were known as 'quarter men' at 10 and 'three-quarter men' at 16 or 17.

The deep mines of the west began to use winding gear to lift coal to the surface. In Fife and the Lothians pits were shallow and women and girls carried coal to the surface on their backs in large creels.

Little Margaret Leveston could carry 25 kg when she was six, and another girl, Jane Johnston, carried 100 kg when she was fifteen.

Children like Rebecca Sim, aged 11, were harnessed to coal waggons with ropes and chains. Her task, with her sister, was

Alexander Stewart's collar.

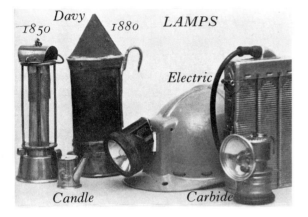

David Allan's 1780 picture of a shed at Lead-hills, Lanarkshire, where boys break lumps of lead ore for smelting in a furnace. Lead miners ceased to be serfs sooner than coal miners — largely because skilled workers had to be attracted from a distance for the processing. In 1780 most industry was on a small scale. Large concerns included Leadhills, the Carron Iron-works and some coal mines.

to pull a waggon weighing 350 kg. Big brother George, aged 14, helped them 'up the brae'.

Women and children were banned from mines in 1842. Janet Cumming, 11, described at an enquiry how she had been a coal bearer for two years, collecting the coal and carrying a 50 kg creel. The roof was so low that she had to bend both back and knees to pass along, and often the water in the tunnel came above her calves. She worked from 5 a.m. to 5 p.m. but on Fridays she worked all night till Saturday noon.

George Reid, aged 16, had hewn coal since he was 10. He found it 'horrible sore work' wielding a pick in a seam 66 cm high. The 9-year-old boys employed at Carron worked in front of the scorching furnaces, often burned by sparks and hot metal and found life in the ironworks just as bad.

Coalface in 1910.

Modern shearer loader at the coalface.

One of the few handloom weavers still working in the nineteenth century at Kirriemuir. His equipment looks traditional and well used.

The main room of the weaver's cottage at Kilbarchan, Renfrewshire, with the bed recess found in many Scottish homes.

A holiday outing for the more prosperous workers in the 1830s. They head for the countryside in a variety of conveyances.

Eighteenth-century handweavers had been the best paid workers in Scotland, working only four days a week and owning their own houses. They dressed like the upper classes in long gilt-buttoned coats, ruffled shirts, smart knee breeches and powdered wigs. Life for thousands of them became grim as farm workers made redundant by new farm machinery, dispossessed highlanders and Irish immigrants came in search of work. Weavers were now so badly paid that they had to move into slum quarters and dress in rags.

The best paid textile workers now were the male cotton spinners who had the strength and skill needed to handle heavy machinery.

In the 1820s they began to earn good wages, enough to rent a decent room and kitchen house and to fill it with mahogany furniture: a proper bedstead, table and chairs, chest of drawers, china cupboard and book-shelf. A prize possession was a grandfather clock. Their families ate well, with fresh meat for dinner and luxuries such as tea, coffee, sugar and white bread.

The cotton spinners kept wages high by forming unions. They knew employers would cut their wages if there were more spinners than jobs. There were often bitter riots as they used violence to stop non-union men entering the trade.

They had seen what happened to the handweavers when too many newcomers came into the industry.

Conditions were specially bad for the women and children in the smaller mills. In James Kirkland's mills at Dunfermline the linen was kept damp so that it would not snap. His workers, girls between 10 and 14, worked a 12 hour day

Pulleys and driving belts feed power to the looms in a weaving mill in 1843. By this time the Factory Acts had banned the employment of children under 13 and appointed inspectors to see that the regulations were carried out.

standing barefooted on a wet, dirty flagged floor, their clothes soaking wet, continuously sprayed by the water thrown off from the machines.

Mill hours were long and employers sometimes cheated by altering the clocks to suit themselves. Even in good mills the continual standing gave workers varicose veins and children working in a temperature of over 24°C suffered dreadful accidents. Cogs and pulleys did enormous damage when ragged clothes, fingers, arms and hair got tangled in the machinery.

It was better in the bigger mills at New Lanark, Catrine, Deanston or Stanley in Perthshire. Here the employers kept the mills clean, built houses, churches and schools. In New Lanark, Robert Owen, David Dale's son-in-law, encouraged adult education, organised the workers to clean their houses of bugs, lice and fleas and opened a co-operative shop in the village.

Robert Owen (1771–1858) believed that good conditions would make people good. He wanted people to co-operate. He was ahead of his time but his ideas inspired co-operative societies, trade unions and socialist communities.

Owen's New Lanark school for children of 2–10 years was a pattern for the future.

Canal diggers were known as 'navigators'. Later, other construction workers were called 'navvies'.

24 Nineteenth Century: INDUSTRIAL WORKERS

More people moved into the coal fields and industrial towns all through the nineteenth century. They came from the highlands and islands, from overcrowded lowland farms and above all they came from Ireland.

Steamboats made the crossing easy when the Belfast–Portpatrick services opened in 1818. By 1841 over 125 000 Irish immigrants had settled in Scotland, mostly in the west. An even bigger flow came in 1845 and 1846 when the potato crop failed and brought starvation to Ireland. Thousands of Irish died, over a million and a quarter sailed to America and about 115 000 came to Scotland. In 1851 Irish-born people made up 15% of the population of the west of Scotland, and 18% of the people of Glasgow.

Many found jobs as 'navvies' on the new railways which began to cover the country in the 1840s, linking all the outlying parts of Britain together as never before. Others swelled the population of the lowlands, which grew from 1 608 420 in 1801 to 2 888 742 in 1851 and 4 472 103 in 1901. The people who came to the mining villages and cities found little comfort, bad housing and few amenities.

In mining villages the colliery owners built long rows of 2-roomed houses, without sanitation or water supply. The houses soon became horribly over-

Tall closely built Glasgow tenements in 1868 blocked out daylight and clean air.

High School Wynd, Edinburgh, in 1837, one narrow overcrowded street of the 'Old Town'.

crowded, for many of the incomers were single men and as many as fourteen might lodge with a family who rented a colliery house.

Mining villages were rough places, without schools or churches and the only shop belonged to the mine-owner, who often sold on credit at high prices and made large profits from the sale of cheap whisky. At the same time the windswept mining villages were often healthier than the crowded cities.

Town workers ran greater health risks than their ancestors though their one-roomed tenement houses were no more crowded than country cottages and were probably warmer, drier and less smoky. City dirt and poor food shortened the lives of many. Doctors soon noticed that

By contrast, mid-twentieth-century houses at Cumbernauld New Town, famous for its open layout and the skilful use of trees.

fever epidemics hit hardest at the poor. Upper-class Edinburgh citizens in the early nineteenth century lived on average 47 years, but labourers only 26 years.

Moray Place, Edinburgh, from an engraving of 1831. In the New Town, wealthy people were able to live in spacious houses well laid out in streets, squares and crescents pleasing to the eye – with gardens to make them more so.

Libberton Wynd, Edinburgh, in 1854. Seventy years before, Robert Burns met his friends in Dowie's Tavern, here renamed after the poet.

All the big cities had their slum districts but Glasgow and Edinburgh had the worst. In Glasgow the tenements were built so close together that many rooms never got any direct sunlight. Filthy closes led to foul stairs, dirty corridors and one-roomed houses, divided up by box beds and sometimes holding more than one family.

Sanitation was non-existent. People in the upper houses poured away their liquid waste into a tank outside the stair window. The wooden drain pipe was not connected to drain or sewer, however, and its contents simply splashed on to the back court.

In Edinburgh the great gulf between rich and poor was shown in the Old and New Towns. A wealthy lawyer in 1830 had his own four-storeyed house, with servants' quarters in the basement and

This cartoon shows a lecturer demonstrating a scientific experiment at the Andersonian Institute, Glasgow, in the 1820s. Parish schools had always catered for girls as well as boys and it is interesting to see a number of women in the class.

Shuttle Row, now a memorial to Livingstone. A table in an upstairs one-room house was his study until, at 23, he moved to Glasgow.

dining room, drawing room, library, nursery and bedrooms arranged on the upper floors. One Old Town tenement in the 1860s, the Middle Meal-Market Stair, had five floors also, each with 11 or 12 rooms and contained 56 families, a total of 248 people. There was no tap, sink or toilet in the whole building.

Crowded living conditions did not stop determined people working for a better life. The industrial age brought new ideas and opportunities to many.

David Livingstone, for example, was born in a one-roomed house in Shuttle Street, Blantyre, in a tenement near James Menteith's cotton mill. The house was one of twenty-four opening off from a spiral staircase.

His father made his living selling tea from door to door. A religious man, a Sunday School teacher, he was too poor to keep David at school after the age of ten, and David went to work in the mill. He was a strong boy and stood up well to the long hours, 6 a.m. to 8 p.m. and at night he attended school for two hours. By day he kept his Latin book propped up on the machine as he worked.

By the age of 23 he had saved enough money for a 2-year course at the Andersonian Institute, Glasgow. Here, and in London with help from a missionary society, he qualified as a medical missionary and by the age of 28, in 1841, he was ready to set out for Africa to begin his work as missionary and explorer.

Henry Bell's 'Comet', launched in 1812 at Helensburgh, was the first really successful steamship. She plied between Glasgow, Oban, Fort William and Mull – using sails, too.

An 1820 painting of the steamship 'Majestic', built at Greenock to carry mails and passengers between Greenock and Liverpool via Portpatrick and Douglas (IoM) in 24 hours.

The 'Cutty Sark' was built at Dumbarton 1869, last of the fast sailing ships (capable of $17\frac{1}{2}$ knots) that raced to bring the new season's tea from China. Now on view in London.

The 'Servia', first steel vessel of the Cunard Line, built in the 1870s. Clyde shipbuilding companies produced their own steel and by 1900 one quarter of the world's steamships.

25 Late Nineteenth Century: WORK & HOME

The inventions and discoveries of the nineteenth century completely changed the way Scottish people earned their living. By the end of Queen Victoria's reign, in 1901, nearly 500 000 workers depended on the heavy industries (mining, iron and steel manufacture, shipbuilding and engineering) compared with only 200 000 in farming, 28 000 in fishing and 16 000 in the textile trade.

Fishing was still important. There were new ports at Ullapool, Tobermory, Wick and Helmsdale. The use of steam helped fishermen, too: steam trawlers began to sail from Aberdeen in 1882 in search of white fish – cod, ling and haddock. In 1898 steam drifters joined the herring fleets operating from Wick, Aberdeen, Fraserburgh and Peterhead.

Industries boomed right through the century, though the pattern of work changed in the 1860s as the cotton trade died out, except in Lanarkshire and Renfrewshire. Shipbuilding and engineering replaced the cotton industries. Whole towns of shipyard workers grew up: Clydebank did not exist in 1861 but had over 30 000 inhabitants within forty years.

The highlands did not share in the

Herring gutters at Wick in 1905. Fishermen's wives and daughters often moved from port to port, as the fishing boats sailed after the shoals of herring. Their job was to gut and clean the fish.

industrial prosperity of the lowlands. The drift from the north and west continued, in spite of Telford's roads and the work of the Highland and Agricultural Society and the British Fishing Society, both founded at the end of the eighteenth century. There were few clansmen left now, as the government found out when it looked for highland recruits at the time of the Crimean War.

Life for the poor people of Victorian Britain was always overshadowed by the fear of unemployment, sickness and old age. A man who lost his job or could not work had to beg for his living or go into a workhouse. People dreaded old age because it meant living as a burden on their children or a half-starved and comfortless life in an institution.

Indeed, life in the late nineteenth century was an endless struggle. When the people of any town or district all worked at the same occupations, a whole community was badly hit by a firm closing down or by a local disaster. This was very true of the mining districts.

The anxious crowd at the Blantyre coalmine after the explosion of 1877. 207 men were killed – the worst mining disaster ever in Scotland.

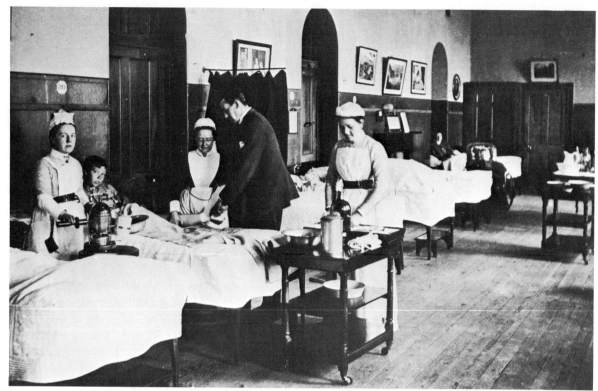

A surgical ward in Aberdeen, 1889. Florence Nightingale's example during the Crimean War had made nursing a well-disciplined and hard-working profession.

James Simpson (1811–1870) began the use of chloroform as an anaesthetic. Surgeons were now able to operate with greater care and undertake more difficult operations.

Joseph Lister, while professor of surgery in Scotland 1860–1877 realised that infection from surgeon's knives and clothes killed many patients. As the first antiseptic he used carbolic acid.

Many women went to work. Worst-off were those who worked in 'sweat-shops', for example, sewing and stitching for clothing manufacturers. Work conditions were foul and wages pitiful, but there were no unions for women, no laws to protect them, and money was needed at home.

Girls went into 'domestic service', as maidservants in middle and upper class homes. In Victorian times, people felt a great gulf lay between those who worked with their hands and those who did not. Everyone who could possibly afford to do so had one or more servants.

Other girls and women found work in offices, for the invention of telephones and typewriters provided new kinds of

Servants' bells at Traquair House. The wealthy employed 'armies' of servants: house staff – butlers, footmen, cooks, maids; personal staff – valets, nurses, governesses; outdoors – gardeners, coachmen, stablemen, gamekeepers.

work very suitable for quick-thinking and quick-fingered girls. Shop girls were needed, too, for the growing number of larger shops that sprang up in the '70s and '80s.

There was work in the new 'services': hospitals wanted nurses and Board Schools needed teachers of all sorts.

The worst social problem was housing, for builders went on with tenement blocks full of 'single-end' and 'room and kitchen' houses even after their health dangers were clear. They built them solidly in stone, with walls up to a metre thick, so

that many still stand today.

Over half the townsfolk lived in these small houses that opened off common stairs in tenement buildings. The tenements started a pattern of crowded living which Scottish people accepted as normal. Even today, Scotland has more crowded houses than any other part of Britain. In 1911, before councils began to build houses, 62·5% of Glasgow people lived in one or two-roomed houses. In other industrial towns of the west (Coatbridge, Wishaw, Kilsyth, Clydebank, Airdrie and Motherwell) nearly 80% of people did so.

Bed recesses built in the walls of kitchens and living rooms made up for the lack of proper bedrooms. They were cosy but diseases like tuberculosis spread rapidly.

In the early part of the century few working-class homes had much furniture. As wages improved people tried to copy middle-class styles as far as they could. The many girls who had been 'in service' knew how their 'betters' lived.

A reconstruction of a working class home (in the Kelvingrove Museum, Glasgow). One room could serve as kitchen, living room, bedroom, nursery and (for people like David Livingstone) as study. Mantelpiece and open shelves are used to display china and metal ornaments.

A reconstruction of a middle class drawing room, with every surface covered with bric-a-brac. The piano, not shown, would also carry a load of china ornaments and framed pictures.

A very upper class dining room at Culzean Castle, home of the Kennedys, earls of Cassilis. The magnificent ceiling is typical of the architect, Robert Adam, who had designed the house for the 10th Earl.

People who could, crammed their homes with furniture, tables with fringed cloths, plant stands, display cabinets, occasional tables littered with framed photographs and ornaments. Women spent hours with feather dusters and polish to keep the whole display in order.

Living in tightly packed tenements was not very healthy but it often led to a great feeling of companionship among neigh-bours. Very often neighbours were rela-tives as well, since different generations (grandparents, parents and children) lived in the same building or the same street.

This companionship was strengthened by the way the men's work was done in shipyards, foundries and mines where they worked in gangs or teams. Men came to rely upon a workmate's skill, strength and experience – and working friendships were carried over into leisure hours.

Working men met in the same public house or at the same street corner, followed the same sporting interests, supported the same football teams and paid their dues to the same branch of the Trade Union.

For women running their own homes and for girls in domestic service there was plenty to do.

Cleaning was a full-time job. Industrial towns were filled with grime and greasy soot from coal fires and factory chimneys. No matter where one lived dust or mud was tramped in from the unpaved streets. Women's long skirts and petticoats soon got dirty so that washing was a heavy task. Drying clothes was another problem; kitchens were often filled with steaming clothes hung on lines.

Cooking called for special skills. Coal fires had to be banked at just the right height for simmering and stewing – and for baking if the housewife was lucky enough to have a kitchen range with an oven.

Shopping took up a great deal of time because there were no frozen foods and few that were packaged or tinned. Women had to shop daily because food kept in the stuffy houses went bad very quickly.

As steamships brought cheap wheat from Canada, bacon from Denmark and meat from Argentina in refrigerated ships, poorer people began to eat meat and bread – welcome additions to porridge, potatoes, herring, broth and the economical Scottish dishes such as haggis and sheep's head.

The most popular shops for poor and

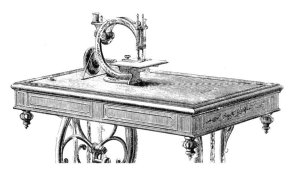

From the advertisement of 1862: From numerous examples of the Sewing Machine exhibited we select the one that has been best subjected to the influence of Art; it is, indeed, a very handsome piece of drawing room furniture.... It is certainly the best of the candidates for public favour ...

Lipton's first shop in Stobcross Street.

Staff outside a tobacconist's and general shop in Airdrie. The name of the shop and the striped pole above the door suggest that there was a barber's in the back room.

Italian ice cream vendors carried on the old tradition of street trading and the ice cream (cheaper than café ice cream) was called hokey pokey. French onion men toured till recently.

thrifty people were those run by Co-operative Societies. These kept prices low by buying in bulk and paid back their profits in 'dividends'.

The idea of co-operatives, like that of trade unions, had come from the active mind of Robert Owen of New Lanark.

There was also a new type of shop whose success depended on the fast transport which linked Scotland with countries overseas. The new shops were 'multiple stores', chains of grocery shops owned by one firm. They kept prices low by buying direct from farmers in Ireland, Denmark and America.

Lipton's and Cooper's of Glasgow were among the first of these stores. Thomas Lipton's first shop was in Stobcross Street, and within a few years he had shops all over Britain. People were attracted by his use of advertising which included stunts such as the scattering of leaflets from balloons and the parade through the streets of giant cheeses pulled by elephants.

Cooper's was also founded in 1871, by Thomas Bishop. His shops were very advanced and his Sauchiehall Street shop was the first in the country to have electric lighting.

26 Late Nineteenth Century: SOCIAL LEGISLATION

After 1856 each county and burgh had to provide a police force, after the pattern of the large burghs or the metropolitan Peelers or Bobbies set up by Sir Robert Peel in 1829. The frock coat and stove pipe hat are a reminder that British police are not soldiers but civilians.

This view of Glasgow in the 1870s shows that water carts still served some parts of the city before water taps were installed at street corners and inside houses.

By 1830, many intelligent and educated people of all classes realised that the government was not running the country properly. Members of Parliament were men of considerable property or wealth and were elected by others of the same kind. They did not understand the needs of the rest of the people, two-thirds of whom now worked in some kind of industry.

The Reform Act of 1832 gave another half million men the right to elect Members of Parliament. Although they were not poor themselves they soon began to choose Members who understood better what was wrong with living and working conditions in towns and factories.

One of the first important Acts swept away the old Scottish Town Councils, made up of merchants and wealthy guild members. Householders in the 79 burghs now elected the councillors they wanted and the Act gave Councils the right to raise their own local taxes, rates.

They spent the money of paving, lighting, laying sewage pipes, bringing in clean water supplies and setting up police forces on the model of Glasgow (1800) and Edinburgh (1805).

Dreadful outbreaks of cholera in the 1840s made Councils move fast in piping water from mountain lochs. Edinburgh Corporation build reservoirs in the Pentland Hills and in 1851 Glasgow Water Board laid a 42 kilometre pipeline from Loch Katrine.

Glasgow Cross in the 1850s. Robert Frame started the first horse-drawn omnibus service in 1845, between Bridgeton and Anderston. Electric lighting began to replace gas in 1893.

Aberdeen Fire Brigade in 1875, with a (horse-drawn) steam-operated pumping engine (p. 121).

Life in the towns improved a great deal as local authorities worked to provide better amenities and services. The big towns, Glasgow, Edinburgh, Dundee and Aberdeen, led the way in providing clean water supplies, sewage and drainage, parks baths, libraries, museums, wash-houses (which were very popular and well used) and hospitals.

There had been gas lighting in some towns since 1818. Gas supplies were gradually improved to provide more homes with gas, although everyone could not afford to install it.

As towns became bigger it became harder to travel between work and home. Private companies began to run 'omnibus' services in the 1870s. By the end of the century the local corporations took them over as public services. Glasgow electrified its tramway system in 1898, beginning a famous tram service which lasted into the 1960s. The old trams travelled along metal tracks in the middle of the street with space at the sides of the street for other vehicles. Many towns owe their wide streets to the tramlines.

Further Reform Acts in 1867 and 1884 gave all men over 21 the right to vote and to do so by secret ballot. (Women did not

Arthur James Balfour (1848–1930) was born of a wealthy family. He became a Conservative Member of Parliament in 1874 and Prime Minister in 1902. Though an eminent British statesman, he was much disliked by many Scots.

get the right to vote until 1918. They were supposed to busy themselves with their homes and children.)

When all men had the right to vote they took a keen interest in politics and argued about the merits and speeches of the Conservative leader, Benjamin Disraeli, and the Liberal leader, William Gladstone. Both the Conservative and Liberal parties were responsible for Acts that improved conditions for the poor.

The Trade Unions flourished in the 1870s and many educated working men discussed how the working classes could form their own party. This was done in 1893 under the leadership of Keir Hardie; by 1906 there were 29 members of the Independent Labour Party in Parliament.

There were 24 'Lib-Labs' as well, who supported both Liberal and Labour views. Between 1906 and 1911 a great number of new Acts of Parliament changed life enormously for industrial workers and their families.

When a Liberal government's reforms gave Old Age Pensions, Unemployment Pay and Sickness Benefits, they lifted a cloud of misery from many people's lives.

'Last Tram to Maryhill', a humorous sketch by Harvey Lambeth. In 1909 Glasgow's electrified tram cars carried 226 948 290 passengers.

James Keir Hardie (1856–1915) was selling newspapers in Lanarkshire at the age of 7 and working in the mines at 10. He educated himself at night school. He formed a Labour Party in 1888 and became a Member of Parliament in 1892.

A variety of fashionable 'Sunday' clothes.

David Stow's 'Uncovered School Room' in 1826. Children used maypoles, skipping ropes, garden tools and building materials for some activities. Stow spread his radical ideas on education through a demonstration school and the first teacher training college, but they spread slowly.

One famous Act of Parliament was the Education Act of 1872 which set up Board Schools for all children between 5 and 13.

Before 1872 there were simply not enough schools. In the 1860s one-sixth of Scottish children had no chance of getting to school at all: in Glasgow the figure was higher – 50%. Magistrates, ministers and businessmen worried about the terrible ignorance they saw round them. Sheriff Watson started 'Ragged Schools' for the poor in Aberdeen in 1841 and Dr. Guthrie did the same in Edinburgh in 1847. David Stow of Glasgow went even further and after starting a Sunday School and a day school he set up the first Training College for Teachers in the whole of Britain.

The new schools of 1872 were known as 'Board Schools' because they were built by School Boards (committees) elected by the ratepayers.

Board Schools gave keen pupils the chance of moving into trades and professions that called for a high level of education. At first, Board Schools concentrated on little more than the '3 Rs' but by 1892 they had won the right to present pupils for the new Leaving Certificate, first set up in 1887.

This called for a good knowledge of subjects such as English, Arithmetic, Mathematics, French, German, Latin, Greek and, later, Science. Those who passed might go to a university or college or train for some professional post. By 1892, also, girls were allowed to attend universities in Scotland and to take degrees.

The school-leaving age was raised to 14 in 1883 but until 1901 many children left

The University of Glasgow, founded in 1451, moved from Rotten Row (see the illustration on page 70) to the High Street in 1561 (see the illustration on page 125) and, three centuries later in 1870, to an impressive new building at Gilmorehill.

early. They could leave as soon as they had worked their way from Standard I to Standard V, and they could study part time only if they had passed Standard III. The examinations were held at the end of each year and a pupil had to pass the Standard examination before going into a higher class.

Many left early because they were poor and because the work they were going to do did not call for book knowledge. Even today nearly 80 % of Scottish workers are employed in manual occupations (skilled, semi-skilled and unskilled). In the nineteenth century the percentage was even higher.

The school 'lines' at Hamilton board school in 1900. Many children went barefoot to school in summer but wore boots in winter – some went barefoot all the time.

27 Late Nineteenth Century: TIME OFF

Local fairs had provided entertainment since the Middle Ages, both in town and country. The sketch of Glasgow Fair in 1825 shows the kind of occasion that people enjoyed in the days before the coming of cinemas, radio and television. Peep-shows, theatres, acrobats, circuses, menageries and prize fights drew people to local fairgrounds. Many burghs had

Detail from the same picture of Glasgow Fair 1825 as on page 115. There were very few theatres because the Kirk disapproved of them – but music hall was to become popular later.

Cockfighting was popular till 1849 when it was banned (and later in some places). Teachers ran cockfights and kept the dead birds for food.

regular race-meetings as well. The 'Fair Fortnights' are still taken as local holidays today.

As early as 1770 fashionable people began to copy George III's visits to the seaside and Helensburgh was built as a resort for the wealthy. Largs, Dunoon and Rothesay grew up in the same way. Railways and steamboats opened up the whole Clyde area for holidays.

As life became easier for most people – working hours were cut and Saturday afternoon became a regular half holiday – townsfolk followed the example of the rich and flocked to enjoy the seaside and the country. Glaswegians went 'doon the watter' to seaside resorts on the Clyde. Edinburgh people made Portobello a favourite resort and each fishing village attracted holiday-makers.

Golf was the first game to be organised on a national basis. The Royal and Ancient Club of St. Andrews had laid down the rules in 1754 and the first Open Championship was held in 1860. Football followed, when the Scottish Football Association was founded in 1873. Queen's Park won the first Scottish Cup.

The first football clubs were all amateur but by the end of the century many teams used professional players. All the clubs attracted eager local support. Glasgow Rangers was started in 1872, playing on Glasgow Green, and its famous rival, Celtic, in 1883.

Village sports had always been popular – quoits, bowling and curling as well as football. Now they all became organised in national leagues, with away and home

Members of the Royal and Ancient Golf Club of St. Andrews about 1907. Some form of golf had been popular since the Middle Ages (see page 50) when, however, the ground was all rough.

The 'Ben More' leaving the Broomielaw, Glasgow, to sail 'doon the watter' to one of the Clydeside resorts, such as Dunoon. Dress on these occasions was still very formal.

Celtic playing Rangers in the final of the Glasgow Cup at Cathkin Park, Glasgow, on 26 May 1895. Celtic won. It was evidently too expensive for many people to buy tickets for the covered seats.

matches and competitions. Large crowds began to follow national contests and to travel to see their favourite teams play.

Cycling became a popular sport and pastime with the invention of the 'safety bicycle'. People began to see their own country for the first time. Amongst other things, people cycled to sports meetings and to the Highland Games which became very popular after Queen Victoria and Prince Albert attended the Braemar Gathering in the '50s.

The first Scottish motor-car, the Arrol-Johnston, built in 1895. Its top speed on the flat was 17 mph and Johnston was fined for speeding. Compare with Slezer's carriage scene (p. 83).

28 Late Nineteenth Century:
LIFE FOR THE WELL-TO-DO

Rich people had begun moving out of dirty city centres just after the middle of the eighteenth century.

Some built mansions in the country – sometimes on the grandest scale – copying the great houses of the nobility such as Hopetoun House. Others built smaller houses, the size according to their wealth. It took armies of servants to run all the houses but wages were low and there was never any shortage of butlers, footmen and maids.

Rich Dundee businessmen lived in Newport, across the Tay, and travelled by ferry between home and work. Aber-deen had its select residential area in the precincts of the old college and Edinburgh its New Town. From Glasgow new suburbs expanded south and west.

Fine villas were built in the outer suburbs of cities. Fanciful 'Gothic' styles appeared which often sprouted pin-nacles, turrets and spires. They were, however, beginning to offer their owners real comfort. Kitchens had coal-burning ranges with ovens, hot plates and water heaters. Some upper-class homes had gas cookers as early as the 1850s and gas lighting was common.

The better houses had baths and bath-

'Gothic' villa at Wemyss Bay, Firth of Clyde.

Sportsmen of the 1880s, stalking deer.

Sir Walter Scott (an Edinburgh lawyer) did much enthusiastic research into old tales, particularly those of the border country. In Scotland his poems and novels aroused new interest in national history – and all over Europe his stories and descriptions of natural scenery influenced the writing of novels. His first (verse) stories included 'The Lay of the Last Minstrel', 'Marmion' and 'The Lady of the Lake' and were followed by a series of novels beginning with 'Waverley' in 1814.

rooms though portable tubs and basins were more usual until the twentieth century. It was cleanliness that often marked off the well-to-do from the poor. 'Cleanliness is next to Godliness' was a favourite saying as preachers, teachers and politicians encouraged the working classes to model themselves on the 'upper' classes. Many people were convinced that if everyone worked hard, saved money and kept clean the whole country would be free of misery and disorder.

Walter Scott's poems and novels had given his readers a new and romantic view of Scotland and Scottish history. Travellers flocked to see the rugged highlands and picturesque glens.

When Queen Victoria and Prince Albert built a 'romantic' castle at Balmoral in 1855 landowners copied their example and built mansions in the Scottish Baronial style. When Albert designed his own tartan they took to wearing kilts, also.

Many highland estates became the playgrounds of the very rich. Stocked with deer, they catered for shooting parties from the south of Scotland and from England which came in search of deer and grouse among the deserted moors and mountains.

Clan chiefs and their sons no longer had any power. They were 'respectable landed gentry', often educated at English public schools.

The Broomielaw, Glasgow, in the 1880s. Traffic was still horse-drawn, lighting was by gas. Glasgow was a thriving city with a growing population – many of whom still lived in poverty among the city slums.

29 POSTSCRIPT TO THE NINETEENTH CENTURY

In the two hundred years that had passed since John Slezer published his drawings, Scotland had become a country of town dwellers. Seventy-five per cent of the population of $4\frac{1}{2}$ million now lived in towns and large villages: of these, $1\frac{1}{2}$ million lived in the five big cities – Glasgow, Edinburgh, Dundee, Aberdeen and Paisley.

Certainly the last years of the nineteenth century showed that the Industrial Revolution could bring a better way of life for rich and poor alike. Britain grew steadily richer because of her industrial exports and her great empire which stretched over a quarter of the globe. She was involved in few wars.

Steam, gas and electricity made possible all sorts of labour-saving appliances which helped to make lives easier and more varied. The nineteenth-century way of life continued until 1914, when World War I broke out. Motor cars and telephones had certainly appeared in the nineteenth century and the first aeroplane flew in 1903, but the impact of these inventions came after 1914.

30 A GLANCE AT THE TWENTIETH CENTURY

The twentieth century has been so packed with changes that it needs a whole book to itself.

Like the rest of the people of Britain, Scots were badly affected by the two World Wars and by the slump in industry that came between them. Scots were, in fact, hit hardest as so many worked in the heavy industries. At one time 400 000 people were out of work, 30 % of the total labour force.

Since then governments have worked to provide each area with a wide range of light industries so that if one factory closes its workers can find jobs nearby.

One of the most promising solutions to the problems of working and housing has been the building of New Towns such as Glenrothes, Cumbernauld, Livingston, East Kilbride and Irvine.

They are specially planned to provide a variety of work (for both men and women) and housing suitable for different sizes and sorts of families. Each New Town has its own transport services and links with main highways and airports. It contains all the amenities of a town: shops, churches, libraries, cinemas, community halls, hospitals, restaurants, cafés, public houses, parks, playing fields and open spaces.

Electricity (here cleanly produced by the power of water falling over the dam at Pitlochry) has completely changed conditions.

The original apparatus used in the 1920s by John Logie Baird, the pioneer of television.

Aerial view of houses at Livingston New Town. ►
Authorities provide a variety of sizes and styles to suit different needs – one-storey and two-storey houses, small (five-storey) blocks of flats.

An American cargo 'plane at Prestwick airport, the most important international airport in the country. The speedy transport of goods and passengers between towns and countries would have astonished people of even a century ago – as would the speed with which news is transmitted from the other side of the world by telephone, wireless and television.

If their industries prosper and if they can re-create a genuine sense of community, New Towns may provide the best plan for living in the Scotland of the future.

In the meantime, authorities are faced with problems whose roots lie deep in history. One of the problems arises from the way that the population is grouped. For two hundred years people have drifted into the central lowland belt in search of work so that now the majority of people are crammed into one portion of the land.

This concentration of people in one area has made the cities full of old and over-crowded houses. Many of the industries that attracted people to the cities no longer exist.

It is always unwise to predict what will happen in the future. The discovery of oil off the Scottish coast, the entry of Britain into the European Common Market and the re-zoning of local government all suggest possible developments.

Scots are better equipped technologically to satisfy their wants than any of their ancestors. The future depends on how well they use the skills and knowledge inherited from the past.

Trays of scampi being brought ashore at Oban. They would perhaps be recognised today by the 'strand loopers' of the Middle Stone Age.

Books

Cameron, A. D.: History for Young Scots, Volume II *Oliver & Boyd* 1963
Cameron, A. D.: Living in Scotland 1760–1820 *Oliver & Boyd* 1969
Macphail, I. M. M.: A History of Scotland for Schools Book 2 *Arnold* 1954
Nichol, N.: Glasgow from Earliest Times to the Present Day *Black* 1969
Nichol, N.: Glasgow and the Tobacco Lords (Then and There) *Longman* 1966
Barclay, J. B.: Edinburgh from Earliest Times to the Present Day *Black* 1965
Lobban, R. D.: The Clansmen *Oxford University Press* 1969
Stevenson, W.: The Jacobite Rising of 1745 (Then and There) *Longman* 1968
Fidler, K.: The '45: Culloden *Lutterworth* 1973
Boog-Watson, E. J.: An 18th Century Highlander *Oxford University Press* 1965
Raine, M.: Culloden *Wheaton* 1967
Scarfe, G.: A Highland Glen About 250 Years Ago *Longman* 1967
Shapiro, H.: Scotland in the Days of Burns (Then and There) *Longman* 1968
Brash, R.: Glasgow in the Tramway Age (Then and There) *Longman* 1971
McKechnie, K.: A Border Woollen Town in the Industrial Revolution (Then and There) *Longman* 1968
Ritchie, W. K.: Edinburgh in its Golden Age (Then and There) *Longman* 1967
Allen, E.: Victorian Children ⎫
Baker, M.: Food and Cooking ⎪
Hoare, R. J.: The Story of Aircraft ⎬ (Junior Reference Books) *Black*
Leighton, P.: Coins and Tokens ⎪
Unstead, R. J.: Travel by Road ⎪
White, P.: Fairs and Circuses ⎭

For visual material
History at Source: Scotland: The Rise of Cities 1694–1905 ⎫ *Evans*
            Scotland: Revolution in Industry 1703–1913 ⎭

Aerial view of Grangemouth oil refinery and chemicals plant.

Museums

Readers would be well advised to explore the possibilities of museums, libraries and art galleries in their area (many of which are not well publicised). Towns in the following list certainly have one or more and many will have castles and mansions nearby which may be of interest.

Aberdeen	Elgin	Largs
Airdrie	Falkirk	Lerwick
Alloway	Forfar	Meigle
Annan	Forres	Melrose
Anstruther	Fort George	Millport
Arbroath	Fort William	Milngavie
Auchindrain	Glamis	Montrose
Ayr	Glasgow	Nairn
Banff	Glencoe	Newtonmore
Biggar	Glenesk	North Berwick
Blair Atholl	Greenock	Paisley
Blantyre	Hamilton	Peebles
Brechin	Hawick	Perth
Bruar Falls	Inverkeithing	Peterhead
Buckie	Inverness	Rothesay
Campbeltown	Inverurie	St. Andrews
Castle Douglas	Jedburgh	Saltcoats
Ceres	Kilbarchan	Selkirk
Coldstream	Kilmarnock	South Queensferry
Cromarty	Kingussie	Stirling
Culross	Kinnesswood	Stranraer
Dalry	Kinross	Strathaven
Dumfries	Kirkcaldy	Stromness
Dunblane	Kirkcudbright	Tain
Dundee	Kirkintilloch	Thurso
Dunfermline	Kirkoswald	Withorn
Ecclefechan	Kirkwall	Wick
Edinburgh	Kirriemuir	

Index

Acknowledgements

The author and publisher would like to thank the following individuals and organisations for permission to reproduce their pictures in this book:

Aberdeen Public Libraries 105a, 107c, 144a, 150b
Aberdeen University Library 136a, 155c
Aerofilms 159c
Airdrie Public Library 148a
Earl of Ancaster 82
Birmingham Museum & Art Gallery 124b
Bodleian Library 93a
British Airports Authority 160a
British Museum, Trustees of 90a, 94, 96a, 109c, 123a
British Petroleum facing p. 160
British Waterways Board 138
Sir John Clerk of Penicuik Bt 84a
Crown Copyright: Royal Commission on Ancient Monuments, Scotland Title page, 87c, 91b, 95a, 106a
Cumbernauld Development Corporation 139c
Dumfries Burgh Museum 111a & b
Edinburgh City Libraries 85c, 87b, 139b, 140b, 143a, 155b, 157b
Edinburgh, University of 144c
Ferranti Ltd 122a
Glasgow Art Gallery 113
Glasgow Museum of Transport 156
A. R. B. Haldane from *Drove Roads of Scotland* published by David & Charles 99a, b & c
Director, Hamilton Burgh Museum 153b
Huntly House Museum, Edinburgh 110c
Jarrold Colour Publications 87d, 93c, 145a
Livingstone Memorial, Blantyre 141b & c
Mansell Collection 89b, 93b, 126, 131, 134b, 137a, 142c, 143b, 147a, 149a, 150c, 154b
Mary Evans Picture Library 123c, 136c, 147b
Mitchell Library, Glasgow 89c, 108a, 124a, 125c, 130a, 131a, 133b, 139a, 142a & d, 148b, 149b, 150a, 152, 153a, 155a, 157a
National Army Museum 92b
National Coal Board of Scotland 135b, d & e
National Galleries of Scotland 86, 88a & b, 97a & b, 98a, 103c, 104a & c, 107b, 115a, 117a & b, 119a, 121a, b & c, 123b & e, 127a, 137b, 144b, 157c

National Library of Scotland 98b, 101a & b, 102, 103a & b, 105b, 112a, b & c, 116b, 117d, 120a, 121d, 133a, 134a
National Maritime Museum 142b
National Museum of Antiquities of Scotland 91c & d, 92a, 96b, 114a & b, 135a
National Portrait Gallery 151a
National Trust for Scotland 136b, 146b
Old Glasgow Museum, Glasgow Green 145b, 146a
Peter Baker Photography 159a, 160b
Post Office Records 128, 129b & c
Radio Times Hulton Picture Library 100, 108b & c, 119b, 127b, 129d, 130b, 137c, 158
Reading, University of, Museum of English Rural Life 132b
Kenneth Robertson 107a
Science Museum Contents page, 132a & c, 159b
Scottish United Services Museum 104b, 120b
West Highland Museum, Fort William 106b
E. R. Yerbury & Son 148c
116a is reproduced from a picture in a private collection in Scotland

Cover illustrations
Pitlessie Fair
    National Galleries of Scotland
Start of Mail Coach
Washerwomen on Carlton Hill
    Huntly House Museum, Edinburgh
Early washing machine
    Mansell Collection
Oil rig
    Shell International Petroleum Company Ltd
Colliery notice
    National Coal Board of Scotland

Map by Barry Evans